We hold these truths to be self-evident, that all men are created equal, that they are endowed by their Creator with certain unalienable Rights, that among these are Life, Liberty and the pursuit of Happiness. — That to secure these rights, Governments are instituted among Men, deriving their just powers from the consent of the governed, — That whenever any Form of Government becomes destructive of these ends, it is the Right of the People to alter or to abolish it, and to institute new Government, laying its foundation on such principles and organizing its powers in such form, as to them shall seem most likely to effect their Safety and Happiness.

I0026998

—excerpt from Declaration of Independence

I dedicate this book to the many sincerely concerned Americans I have known who realized that just voting does not satisfy our responsibility as citizens of a free society and took the step to become actively involved. Whether they put themselves forth as candidates or as volunteers to help good candidates and good causes, it is they who will save our country and our way of life.

Al Lee

Patriotism: Supporting your Country all the time; and, your Government when it deserves it – Mark Twain

Pruning the Fourth Branch
Version 1.0
  revised: 11/23/2012 9:33:15 PM
© 2012 Al Lee & Associates, Inc.
all rights reserved
PO Box 702685, Dallas, TX 75370-2685
www.ReformAdminLaw.org
ISBN: 0971173818
ISBN-13 978-0971173811

ReformAdmin
    Law.org

TABLE OF CONTENTS

1. Foreword

Wesley A. Riddle holds a Bachelor of Science from the U. S. Military Academy at West Point and an M. Phil. with Distinction in Modern History from Oxford University. He is a former Policy Advisor to the Chairman of the Texas Workforce Commission and is currently on faculty at Central Texas College as Professor of Government

...

"Pruning the Fourth Branch" is essential reading for the patriot policymaker. Al Lee brings to light perhaps the single biggest issue that has been largely overlooked by post-World War II pro-Constitution reformers, namely the issue of Administrative Law. He makes clear the reforms that are necessary to be made to it in order to restore our limited constitutional form of government. For, without tackling the Bureaucracy at its root as he describes, there is no institution or political process capable of reigning in the federal government!

Administrative law reform may be the last, but also the most effective, means available to Congress to stop the terrible accretion of power to Washington. Few political observers connect the dots the way Lee has managed to do in his fine and timely study. Even those who have been around politics a long time are likely to learn something new. For instance, he relates how the Supreme Court's decision to uphold the individual mandate provision of the Affordable Healthcare Act effectively de-limits power to Washington and abandons traditional checks and balances—because the decision confers congressional authority for taxation to the Bureaucracy!

Moreover, the decision sets a brand new precedent for fines being considered as taxes. On this basis therefore, every single agency, whether it has a "czar" in charge or not, whether it relates to human activities of education, energy, commerce, environment, health, *whatever*—every single agency of the Bureaucracy may now bypass the Congress and the President to regulate every individual directly, enforcing its regulation by means of a fine, a.k.a. America's new *taxation without representation*.

The Court's decision thus constitutes a modern equivalent of the Stamp Act! For those of you who believe that we are Taxed Enough Already, administrative law reform inevitably must become a critical political objective, because without it there is little recourse to the Constitution or to constitutional limits on the power to tax or on the concomitant powers to control and, as John Marshall pointed out, to destroy.

Wes Riddle

2. About the Author

When the Founders of our country drafted the Constitution, a huge debate ensued over whether or not it would be sufficient protection against tyranny. One group of patriots that we call "Federalists" argued in a series of essays we call the "Federalist Papers" that the Constitution was adequate to protect the people from government expansion. James Madison, John Jay, and Alexander Hamilton authored these essays, all using the pen name "Publius." The opposing view was argued by patriots such as Patrick Henry and Thomas Jefferson, who were exceedingly wary of a strong central government.

In some ways it seems that Publius underestimated the shrewdness of power-hungry government officials and overestimated the will of future generations to remain vigilant against the spread of government powers. If the United States of America falls into tyranny from its own government, as seems all too possible, then Publius will have been proven wrong and a terrible price will be paid by our posterity.

Now we are fighting to make true what Publius optimistically *believed* would be true — that the Constitution would prevail. And I believe we have found a way to use Publius' very own words as a tool to do that.

I am a life-long conservative political activist who has once run for office (unsuccessfully) and has for decades supported political candidates who revere the Constitution. The first candidate I supported was Ronald Reagan in his 1980 campaign and I was fortunate enough to attend his Inaugural Ball. I remember the thrill of feeling that we had turned the country around. But I have come to realize that just electing Conservatives will not be enough to save us. I have become convinced that our federal government has been fundamentally altered in a way designed to render the Constitution impotent. I believe that we must look back over the past one-hundred years to understand what was done and how it was done in order to understand how we must remedy it.

A question I would like you to keep in mind as you delve into this book: If you were given a government that was structurally architected to make it virtually impossible to accumulate tyrannical power; but your objective was to acquire just such power, what would be your first step?

I am not a constitutional scholar. I am merely a concerned citizen who has become impassioned about what I believe to be one of the most important issues we must address. Most of the information I relate in this book I have learned from some of the true conservative political leaders I have known and from research inspired by them. A few of the ideas I propose in this book may be original from me; but most were learned from others. I will try to give attribution wherever I can.

It is for my beautiful children and grandchildren that I am writing this book. May I never have to look into their faces to say I am sorry I did not give my all to preserve their freedom.

3. Introduction

In 2011 our government dispatched US marshals, assisted by Pennsylvania State Troopers and federal agents, to conduct an early-morning raid on an operation that they determined was threatening our security. The raid was the culmination of a year-long campaign that included under-cover agents, sting operations, and surveillance. The target organization had the innocent-sounding name, "Rainbow Farms." This Amish dairy business was — *selling raw milk to natural food enthusiasts.*

In 2012 our government added new regulations that made about one-third of America's electric generation illegal, a move that could drive the cost of electricity for every American through the roof.

In the same year, our government raided and shut down the Gibson Guitar Corporation's guitar manufacture operations because an exporter in India may have mislabelled a shipment of ebony wood that Gibson purchased. A government agent advised Gibson that it might be better if they outsourced some of their labor to avoid the "problem."

When fifty-six brave men met on a hot July day to sign a declaration that pledged their lives, their fortunes, and their sacred honor, do you believe that this sort of behavior by our American government was what they had in mind to establish? Did they struggle through eight years of war against the most powerful nation on Earth for *this*? Did they engage in years of contentious debate to design a new government that would attack its own citizens this way? I do not think so.

The Founders carefully crafted a government with three branches that held one another in check expressly to prevent this sort of perversion of government "of the people, for the people, and by the people," as Abraham Lincoln described it in his "Gettysburg Address." Today, through sleight-of-hand by statist politicians for eight decades, we actually have a **Fourth Branch** of our government. A branch that operates virtually unchecked, allowing the sort of abuses I described above and many, many more.

In this book I will describe how this came to be and how we can fight to right this wrong. I also will explain why this is one of the most critical problems we must address if we are to preserve our liberty.

> "All the armies of Europe, Asia and Africa combined could not by force take a drink from the Ohio or make a track on the Blue Ridge, in a trial of a thousand years. At what point then is the approach of danger to be expected? I answer, if it ever reaches us, it must spring up amongst us. If destruction be our lot, we must ourselves be its author and finisher." – Abraham Lincoln

4. The Problem

Please ask yourself three simple questions:

- Do you believe that the government imposes regulations for your benefit or for its benefit?

- Do you think that the rules and regulations from our government are making America more or less competitive in the world?

- Do you feel more or less secure as you become more dependent on the government?

If you are comfortable with the steady intrusion of government regulation into even the most private aspects of our lives, this book will not interest you. If you are concerned that you are rapidly losing your freedom and believe that we are far along on the path to tyranny, and want to do something about it, please read on!

As we observe the steady encroachment of government into every aspect of our lives we are inclined to instinctively rail about the evil that politicians wreak upon us and the need to elect better men and women to public office—folks who understand that we want to be free and that our country was founded on the principle that individual rights, not the powers of the state, should be paramount.

While I can not argue with the idea that we surely ought to be able to find better people to elect to office than we often have in the past, decades of involvement with the political process have taught me that the expansion of government is more a systemic cancer than the result of any individual or even our current crop of sorry political officials. To be sure, the

DHS classifies ordinary Americans as terrorists

cancer was introduced and is still nurtured by many men and women who hold public office; but by now it has achieved the size and penetration of our political system and society that

enable it to spread and grow with or without the help of bad politicians.

Rules that cripple vital American industries, such as electricity generation, oil & gas production, or automobile manufacturing in the United States are not in the best interests of our economy. Regulations to prevent citizens from selling raw milk, growing their own food, or storing food for emergencies are certainly not what the Founding Fathers envisioned for our nation; but these are merely a small sampling of the thousands of restrictions planned, or already placed upon us without even a credible pretense of their being for our own good. Rather, they are intended to increase our dependency upon government and to prevent self sufficiency among the American populace.

Rules and restrictions that make American workers unable to compete with their foreign counterparts who are not similarly fettered, thereby encouraging outsourcing of every sort of American job, surely would have had no place in the thinking of American statesmen just a few decades ago. But now it seems that our government imposes every impediment they can think up upon our own American industry and workforce.

Many politicians and candidates for office will promise to fight against this usurpation of our rights; but none seems to actually have a plan to solve the problem. At best, they will continue to flail endlessly at a myriad of malicious rules and regulations. But the monster is like the Hydra of Greek mythology; for each head that is lopped off, two more grow back.

To see just how many regulations our federal bureaucracy can create every year, every month, even every day, you can visit the federal government's own website and just tool around.

Note: I make reference in this book to numerous events (recent and historical), laws, and rules. To document them, there are online references that you can access listed at the back of this book. Depending what format your book or eBook is in, you may be either able to click on them as a hyperlink or to copy and paste into your browser. Of course, if you are reading the book on paper, you would have to type the URL into your browser.

On the day I am writing this page, the government website, regulations.gov, reports:

NEWLY POSTED REGULATIONS

- Last 3 Days (198)
- Last 7 Days (486)
- Last 15 Days (1,061)
- Last 30 Days (1,969)
- Last 90 Days (6,215)

That indicates that we will have about 25,000 new regulations added in one year. And I have no reason to believe that the bureaucracy is now churning out regulations at a particularly faster pace than normal, or even that they are producing them as fast as they usually do or are capable of. I am sure that the regulators can push these numbers even higher if they put themselves to the job.

This should make it obvious that to fight against these regulations individually is a hopeless task. The federal regulation machinery can turn them out faster than we can even read them, much less, repeal them in court actions. You would have to win more than sixty (60+) court cases *per day* to just keep pace with the inflow of new regulations. We must find a better way to fight them.

To be fair, not all regulations regulate the private sector or individuals directly. Many regulate the agencies themselves and dictate how they will issue and administer their rules and regulations; but even they can have an adverse effect upon us because the danger is not only the regulations that are imposed; but also how they will be enforced.

The malignant growth of government regulations is a cancer that is choking and smothering the land of liberty our Founders established. In this book I will describe a strategy I propose that, if implemented with persistence and dedication, can stop the spread of this fatal disease and will actually reverse its pernicious intrusion into our lives and businesses. But,

9

implementing it will require more courage and commitment than most of our current crop of politicians possess. Thus, in order to prevail, we must both promote this strategy *and* continue to fight to elect people to public office who both understand the problem and possess the backbone to join the fight to fix it. Then, to reinforce that backbone, we must stand behind them in huge numbers supporting this cause.

The good news is that as we make progress in winning popular support for our mission it will become easier to win over politicians and officeholders; and as we win over those officials, it will be easier to reach more voters with our message to win even greater popular support.

> Politicians usually make grand promises to give us this or that. We often criticize them for not keeping their promises; but ultimately, we may be harmed more by the promises they keep than by the ones they break.

A number of conservative political figures have told me personally that they are sympathetic to our mission for reform and that they *will* help us. You will see some of their names in this book and I will be approaching others at every opportunity. We can take encouragement from the fact that we are not alone. We have already begun to enlist important allies.

5. The Three Branches

The Founding Fathers put much experience and wisdom and many years of thoughtful deliberation into designing and refining the structure of our federal government. They codified it in the Constitution with its Bill of Rights, the most remarkable document of law ever written.

The US Capitol is the home of the Legislative Branch of our government

They clearly defined a government divided into three branches: The Executive, The Legislative, and The Judicial Branches.

The Legislative Branch has the power to make laws, declare war, and coin money; but its foremost function is to serve as a check on The Executive and Judicial Branches. The Executive branch carries out the laws; but its foremost function is to serve as a check on the other two branches. The Judicial Branch interprets laws; but, again, its most important function is to serve as a check on the other two branches. And all three Branches are subordinate to the Constitution.

The Constitution provides a specific oath of office for the President and requires that all other federal and state government officials of every branch "shall be bound by Oath or Affirmation to support this Constitution."

The architecture of our government structure included these built-in "checks and balances" among the divisions of our government so as to

The White House is home of the leader of the Executive Branch

prevent any one Branch from gathering too much power to itself. At least, that was the idea.

The Founders did not intend to establish a national government that would supplant the various State governments already in place. Rather, they intended to create a federation of those States that would leave State powers intact except for a short list of things that they agreed would be better handled by the federation. We call that short list "the Enumerated Powers."

For a century and a half it seemed to work pretty well. The powers of the federal government did grow; but at a very gradual pace with States' powers remaining largely intact.

One significant event a century ago greatly reduced States' powers, though. In 1913 the Seventeenth Amendment to the US Constitution was ratified. It changed the way that US Senators are elected. (Incidentally, in that same year the Federal Reserve Bank was established by Congress and the Income Tax was initiated — a momentous year!)

> Note: In this book you will notice that I never use the term "states rights." That is because the Founders understood a clear distinction between rights and powers. They believed that rights are granted by God and are inalienable. Powers are granted to the Federal Government by the States and to the States by the People, *and can be retracted*. The government has *powers* or *authority*—only citizens have *rights*. The term "states rights" was coined by the Confederacy to justify secession in the Civil War. Without judging whether the southern states were right or wrong to secede, I will say that the issue was whether or not they legally had the *authority*, not the *right*, to do so.

The Constitution defined two chambers of the Legislative Branch. The House of Representatives is known as the "People's House." Representatives are elected directly by popular vote. The Senate is known as "The Upper House." Senators, according to the original Constitution, were elected by the State legislatures. That made US Senators representatives *for the States*.

The Founders could have easily established just one chamber of the Legislature — a "unicameral" legislature — with representatives elected by the People, such as some States now have. Or they could have established two chambers—a "bicameral" legislature—with both elected by the People, as we now have at the federal level after the Seventeenth Amendment. They did not choose either of those options.

I believe that their design of a bicameral legislature with one house elected by the States and one elected by the People was a carefully deliberated measure on the part of the Founders. They knew that the People were often fickle and prone to hasty, emotional judgments driven by their individual personal circumstances at any given moment in time, while States would be more deliberative with a broader and more long-term perspective. By dividing power in the Legislature this way, they created an effective damper on two of the biggest problems of Democracy (our government is not, and never was intended to be, a Democracy—it is a Constitutional Representative Republic). The problems are:

The Supreme Court is the pinnacle of the Judicial Branch

- hasty actions based on momentary circumstances, and

- a tyranny of the majority (two wolves and a sheep voting on what to have for lunch).

They very consciously avoided establishing a Democracy because they knew that it was an unstable form of government that would quickly fall into anarchy and thus lead to tyranny. They understood that a certain amount of government was required to establish individual liberty; but too much government would destroy it.

> "*Government, even in its best state, is but a necessary evil; in its worst state, an intolerable one.*" — *Thomas Paine*

Also, they made a clear distinction between a national government and a federation of the States. As I said earlier, they did not want to establish a national government. They wanted to establish a federation of the States, each of which would continue to be self-governed and sovereign. A national government would have been too powerful and would evolve into a tyrannical oligarchy. They clearly wanted to preserve the powers of the individual States and to have the Federal Government respectful of State sovereignty, but able to combine the strengths of the collective States for purposes of security and orderly coexistence among them.

I might interject here that the word "democracy" is regularly misused these days to describe our form of government. The Founders were adamant regarding the dangers of a democracy and the importance of avoiding creating one. Democracy is an unstable arrangement that has quickly fallen to anarchy, and then to tyranny, every time it has been tried as a political form of government. The misuse of the term is the result of inadequate education (mostly from public schools) regarding our government, our American history, and forms of government throughout world history in general.

Changing the way that Senators are elected seemed to be a move toward a closer tie between them and the people. It was seen as a step closer to Democracy (something the Founders, remember, were careful to avoid), which was appealing to those not familiar enough with history to understand the shortcomings of a pure Democracy. The general expectation was that Senators would become more responsive to popular

Senators were originally elected by the state legislatures

will if they were elected directly by the people. In fact, the opposite probably resulted.

According to the architecture the Founders wisely laid out, the State legislatures could recall a badly-performing Senator. Now, because of the Seventeenth Amendment, there is no practical mechanism to recall a Senator. Since they are elected for six-year terms, they easily entrench themselves into the system so thoroughly that it has become close to impossible to defeat a sitting Senator in an election (odds are 98:2 against when attempted). Even an unpopular Senator will probably get re-elected easily. Mounting a statewide campaign for the US Senate is a very expensive proposition with a very low probability of success unless you have the advantages that come with incumbency.

So, Senators have nearly the equivalent of a lifetime appointment once they are seated. This arrangement does not encourage them to be more responsive to the people. In fact, many of them are as aloof as the ancient kings and queens of fairy tales. For many, their allegiance becomes more aligned with the exclusive club called "The US Senate" and to the federal government itself than it is to their own constituents.

The constitutional method of electing Senators by State legislatures had its problems, to be sure. Senate seats sometimes went vacant for extended periods of time because of bickering within the State legislatures. There were charges of State legislators selling Senate seats. These problems could have been remedied by much simpler means; but a general "populist" mood in the country made direct election by the People seem like an attractive, democratic idea.

So why would preserving, or restoring, sovereignty to States be better than having power consolidated in the national government? Aren't state officials just as susceptible to corruption and abuse of their powers as national officials are? Yes, they are; but with many states to choose from there is actually a competition among them. They compete for productive citizens and businesses that would add economic strength to their states. If one state, for instance, implemented regulations that imposed hardship on businesses, its neighbors would have an economic advantage to attract valuable taxpaying persons and companies away from them. (example: check out California to Texas or New York to Florida migrations) Competition almost always works for the good of the citizens.

I believe that this shift in the *complexion* of our federal Legislature a century ago helped pave the way for an even more wide-reaching change just twenty years later — a change to the actual *structure* of our federal Government.

I do solemnly swear (or affirm) that I will support and defend the Constitution of the United States against all enemies, foreign and domestic; that I will bear true faith and allegiance to the same; that I take this obligation freely, without any mental reservation or purpose of evasion; and that I will well and faithfully discharge the duties of the office on which I am about to enter: So help me God.

—Legislator's Oath of Office

The Executive and Judicial Branches, the Military, and all State offices have similar oaths to support and defend the Constitution as required in Article VI and in Article II, Section 1 of the Constitution.

6. Enumerated Powers

"...a government bureau is the nearest thing to eternal life we'll ever see on this earth!" — *Ronald Reagan*

President Ronald Reagan

Probably the greatest concern the Founders had regarding the future of our country was the fear that the central government would expand to control too much of our citizens' lives and businesses. They clearly understood that powers granted in order to meet the momentary profane demands of the public soon evolved into permanent powers used to control the public. In government especially, the road to Hell is paved with good intentions. To thwart such growth, they specifically itemized the limited powers of the central government. To reinforce that, they added the Ninth and Tenth Amendments to make it perfectly clear that any powers not specifically enumerated in (Article I, Section 8 of) the Constitution were specifically reserved for the States or for the People.

RULE OF LAW

The unique aspect of a republic, as compared to other forms of government, is that it is based on a "Rule of Law." Other forms are actually all based, in one variation or another, on a "Rule of Men." Even a Democracy is the rule of the majority of men on any particular issue. In one of the references I include in this book there is a very effective illustration of the difference between the Rule of Men in a Democracy versus the Rule of Law in a Republic. It uses a lynching under a tree versus a trial in a court of law. The reference is to a short video about the Forms of Government. I recommend it highly.

By codifying the highest order of law in the land into a written Constitution, and by including a strict enumeration of the powers of the central government, and by establishing the three-branch self-checking structure, the Founders tried to do the absolute most they could do to prevent the government they established from degenerating into a tyranny over time. The mere fact that men existed in those "primitive" agrarian colonies who possessed the knowledge of world history, the understanding of human nature, and the grasp of philosophy that was required to produce such a result is quite remarkable.

> *"Power corrupts. Absolute power corrupts absolutely"* – Lord Acton

Although they established a government that was based on the Rule of Law, they knew that the governors would be human beings and that they would possess all the usual human failings. They knew that it was the natural inclination of human governors to try to use their powers to gather more powers to themselves. It is a pattern of behavior that has been displayed over and over throughout human history and will likely continue until the end of human history. By positioning all of the political officials in the new government in one or another of the three branches, each of which was being contained in its ambitions by the other two, they successfully established a system that was rather stable—one that has endured for centuries. But the ingenuity and ruthlessness of ambitious men knows no bounds.

> "*Yet experience hath shown, even under the best forms [of government], those entrusted with power have, in time and by slow operations, perverted it into tyranny.*" – Thomas Jefferson

It was inevitable that eventually some would find a way to circumvent the limits that the Constitution placed upon them.

Note: The Rule of Law is critical to individual liberty. It means that the laws are written and publicly displayed so that citizens may know how they can behave in order to remain in compliance and to avoid punishment. Without that, the governors could arbitrarily make or enforce laws, even retroactive laws, that no citizen could avoid running afoul of. A Rule of Law also means that all citizens are subject to the same laws, which will be enforced uniformly. That includes, ideally at least, persons who happen to be in positions of power at the moment (*nobody above the law*).

---

7. The Fourth Branch

"Never let a crisis go to waste." — spoken by a person whose name I do not wish to appear in my book

As repulsive as the quotation above is, it is a perfect description of the strategy and philosophy of the American political Left. I am sure the statement was not intended for public consumption; but has leaked out. Though this is a quotation of a recently-made statement, that strategy has been in place for many decades.

Almost from the beginning, Presidents and other high government officials worked to manipulate the system to increase their own powers and to expand the power of the government in general. Woodrow Wilson, who had written in defense of expanded government powers like those of Socialist societies and of the obsolescence of our Constitution, used the crisis of World War I to assume dictatorial powers not much unlike those that Fascist leaders, Hitler and Mussolini, would later use in their countries. He believed that the Constitution needed to be re-interpreted for modern times, which would render it a completely meaningless document.

WILSON THE PROGRESSIVE

Although Woodrow Wilson was a member of the Democrat Party, he embraced many of the principles of the Progressive Party, which included such things as a minimum wage and an income tax. Progressivism was offered as the solution to some real problems in American society at the time; sweat shops, monopolies, and poverty, which made it appear to be a populist idea. Ultimately, though it was all about greater government control, especially over business, which made it more akin to Fascism. (I will say more about the nexus between big government and big business throughout this book.)

"Fascism should more properly be called 'corporatism' because it is the merger of state and corporate power." –Benito Mussolini (undeniably an expert on the subject of Fascism)

Wilson's Progressivism had contempt for the system of checks and balances established by our Founders, and for a strict "originalist" interpretation of the Constitution, which he viewed as being outdated.

He was a proponent of a much stronger Executive Branch, believing that a President or Governor should rightfully exercise as much power as he was able to since he obviously had the support of the citizenry. Of course, that would make a President more like the tribal leader of a pure Democracy than the head of one of three branches of government in a Republic.

Progressivism's basic tenet is that government is complex and needs to be run by an elite corps of experts—that means the Progressives themselves, of course. A political scientist, Wilson was revered as just such an expert by his supporters.

> Note: If you can believe that government should be run by experts, it is a very small step to believing that only experts are qualified to choose who will lead us. That means, only certain select persons should be allowed to vote for our leaders. After all, how can the common citizen make a wise choice of an "expert" to be our leader? You can see how easily we will have "progressed" toward having a Ruling Class and a Common Class.

As for the Progressive Party, it was founded by Theodore Roosevelt, formerly a Republican. One of his original objectives was to break up corporate monopolies and trusts, giving him the name "Trust Buster." Unfortunately, Roosevelt's motivations soon transformed into allowing monopolies to endure; but with government regulation—*Regulated Monopolies*. This made government a "partner" in the monopolies. Whenever government is a partner, it is the *senior* partner!

Such a relationship corrupts both the companies and the government. It opens up numerous opportunities for bribery and collusion (crony capitalism) and it eliminates the natural capitalistic motivations to innovate and to improve products and service to customers.

A prime example of how the government-industry nexus stifles progress can be found in the automobile industry of the old Soviet Union. In the 1940's the Soviet Union had only primitive automobile manufacturing capabilities (mostly built for them by Ford in the 1920's), so Fiat, an Italian auto maker, built plants in the USSR to help them to develop their Soviet auto industry.

When the Soviet Union fell in 1991 the Russian auto industry was still manufacturing automobiles that were technologically identical to the Fiats of the 1940's. There had been virtually no improvements or innovation in half a century. In spite of the notoriously poor quality of the vehicles produced and the fact that the Soviet auto industry could only produce enough cars to satisfy about 45% of their demand, the government would not allow imports that would compete with their monopoly.

A loosely related, but interesting story occurs in Cuba, which was overtaken by Communism in 1959. Cuban law forbade citizens to buy any automobile that was not on the road when Castro took power. That means that Cuba is a Mecca for classic car enthusiasts and tourists (not from the US, of course) wanting to take pictures of a society apparently frozen in time. Those Cubans who own automobiles own 1959 or older American models or newer Russian Lada cars (mainly owned by the government) that are more an antique replica car than a modern automobile. In 2011 the Communist government began discussing changes to the law to allow people to buy modern automobiles. One Cuban refugee with connections back in his home island told me that some Cubans have become masters at restoring and maintaining those classic American cars and that there are some real gems driving on country roads down there. I suppose that a nostalgist might see some benefits to government control after all!

In Cuba, a 1959 American automobile is a "newer model"

Many of Wilson's overreaches were later reversed when the war was over. But it was in 1933 that Franklin Delano Roosevelt took advantage of the general fear and chaos created by the

Great Depression to effect a coup that changed the actual *structure* of our federal government.

Since the three-branch structure of our government provided natural forces to make expansion difficult, the ideal strategy to overcome the constitutional limits on federal powers was to create a **Fourth Branch** that did not include such impediments to growth and expansion. Of course, to call it a Fourth Branch of our government would have raised objections from nearly the entire nation, so that description would usually be avoided; but what FDR achieved through his New Deal does in fact create just that. During FDR's seminal presidency over one-hundred agencies and bureaus were created, many by Executive Orders, others by Congressional Acts. Some agencies were even created by other agencies much the way bacteria multiply.

Note: there is a popular notion, promoted by Socialists and Communists, that Fascism is the polar opposite of Socialism or Communism: the "Right" versus the "Left." It is true that Fascist regimes have strenuously fought against Communist regimes in the past. In fact, though, they are nearly identical with the differences being minor and superficial. They fought because they were competing for the same crop of statist-minded followers. Chiefly, Socialism and Communism involve government ownership of the means of production (business and industry), while Fascism and Progressivism involve nominal private ownership but with total government control through regulation. All are actually Statist and feature a powerful central government and a governing class that must be obeyed by the citizenry and by all businesses without question. So, they are really not much different after all, are they?

A PROBLEM FOR EVERY SOLUTION

We know this Fourth Branch of Government by various names, so I will simply call it: "The Bureaucracy." It consists of many federal government agencies, bureaus, departments, or other entities of various names and descriptions staffed and run by officials who are not elected; but are appointed. They all were initially created purportedly to correct some problem, real or fictitious, that the public was told simply must be dealt with by government for our nation to survive.

"Politicians are the same all over. They promise to build bridges even when there are no rivers." — *Nikita Khrushchev*

A few of the problems are genuine; but the vast majority of them are merely excuses for one or many government agencies and programs to exist.

PARTIAL LIST OF NEW DEAL AGENCIES

Initials	Year Created	Agency
AAA	1933	Agricultural Adjustment Act
CAA	1933	Civil Aeronautics Authority (now) Federal Aviation Agency
CCC	1933	Civilian Conservation Corps
CCC	1933	Commodity Credit Corporation
CWA	1933	Civil Works Administration
DRS	1935	Drought Relief Service
DSH	1933	Subsistence Homesteads Division
EBA	1933	Emergency Banking Act
FAP	1935	Federal Art Project (part of WPA)
FCA	1933	Farm Credit Administration
FCC	1934	Federal Communications Commission
FDIC	1933	Federal Deposit Insurance Corporation
FERA	1933	Federal Emergency Relief Administration
FHA	1934	Federal Housing Administration
FLSA	1938	Fair Labor Standards Act
FMP	1935	Federal Music Project (part of WPA)
FSA	1935	Farm Security Administration
FSRC	1933	Federal Surplus Relief Corporation
FTP	1935	Federal Theatre Project (part of WPA)
FWA	1939	Federal Works Agency
FWP	1935	(part of WPA)
HOLC	1933	Home Owners Loan Corporation
NIRA	1933	Federal Writers' Project
NLRA	1935	National Labor Relations Act
NLRB	1934	National Labor relations Board
NRA	1933	National Recovery Administration
PRRA	1933	Puerto Rico Reconstruction Administration
PWA	1933	Public Works Administration
RA	1935	Resettlement Administration
REA	1935	Rural Electrification Administration (now Rural Utilities Service)
SEC	1934	Securities and Exchange Commission

Initials	Year Created	Agency
SSA	1935	Social Security Administration
SSB	1935	Social Security Board (now Social Security Administration)
TVA	1933	Tennessee Valley Authority
USHA	1937	United States Housing Authority
USMC	1936	United States Maritime Commission
WPA	1935	Works Progress Administration

These agencies were empowered by Administrative Law to make rules and regulations and to enforce them, giving them the *force of law*, even though they are not laws. Though some of them had useful purposes (at least initially), this was an effective circumvention of the constitutional limitations on the powers of the central government. Nearly all these agencies were under the Executive Branch, thus giving the President powers never intended by the Founders. But, although they may have been subordinate to the President initially, since agencies survive from President to President, regardless which party happens to be in power, these agencies, and the many hundreds that have been created since, actually ultimately are more powerful than even a President or a Congress.

When we use the term "agency" in this book, we mean any government-created entity that is empowered to make and enforce rules and regulations. The nomenclature may call them an "office," "service," "department," "commission," "administration," "agency," or possibly even something else. They may be cabinet-level departments, or entities established by an Executive Order or by a Congressional Act. Some may even be called "corporation" and might outwardly resemble a private-sector business, but with the backing of the government.

Government agencies have existed since almost the very beginnings of our nation. Prior to the New Deal, though, they were predominantly service organizations, not regulatory bodies. The US Post Office, for example, delivered mail, it did not dictate what you may write in a letter (until Mail Fraud became a crime in 1872). Government regulation was not unheard of prior to the New Deal; but it was very sparingly employed (normally by the State governments, not the Federal government) and only after serious deliberation. The mentality of the nation at the time allowed FDR to hurl government regulations at us with little forethought and less resistance. Some of these new regulations were later declared unconstitutional; but others remain to this date.

Years later, in 1944, FDR enhanced the aura of Constitutional justification for the massive insertion of government into our lives by proposing a "Second Bill of Rights," which were economic, not political, in nature, guaranteeing such things as housing, medical care, jobs, and, of course, Social Security.

> *"You have a problem and you pray it will go away. Then government creates an agency. Now you have two problems and not a prayer that either will go away." – Al Lee*

Imagine a village in some remote area that has a problem with lightning striking their houses and burning them to the ground. They turn to their mayor and ask: "What can the government do for us?." The mayor decides to establish a Commission of Lightning Defense and appoints a Commissioner, Clyde. Clyde spends some time studying the problem and reports that he needs more information, so funds must be allocated to do more research and he will need a few more staff members. After a couple of years of analysis, they determine that because of the location of the village, there would continue to be lightning strikes, so they should require all citizens to have fire extinguishers—and that his office should regularly inspect all fire extinguishers to be sure they comply with their standards. That will require a few more people on his staff, of course. In order to coerce people to have fire extinguishers, Clyde convinces the mayor that his office must be able to levy fines to citizens not in compliance.

The number of fires remains about the same as before, though some of the damage is reduced because of the fire extinguishers. Periodically Clyde issues reports showing that fires from lightning are still a big problem; thus his office is very important to the village. Every once in a while he is able to justify some increase in staffing and compensation, particularly after some especially bad fire occurs.

The fires continue and the government program continues indefinitely. If the fires were to cease, Clyde and his growing staff would have to find other work, of course; so Clyde has no incentive to implement any changes that might actually prevent fires from lightning.

> *If you put the federal government in charge of the Sahara Desert, in five years there'd be a shortage of sand.*—Milton Friedman

Now imagine a different scenario. That same village with the lightning strike fire problem decides to find a way to solve their problem themselves, rather than rely on the government to do it. Citizens meet and discuss it, they search for ideas to try out and decide to do two things: First, they all agree to install lightning rods on their own homes. Some of the citizens have financial issues and can not afford to do that, so the village church decides to take up collections for a fund to help the poorer citizens to install lightning rods on their houses. Avoiding fires is really in everyone's interests after all. Second they agree to recommend to all residents that they have a fire extinguisher. The church makes little pamphlets available to everyone to promote having a fire extinguisher in their homes. In this scenario virtually everyone comes out ahead (except maybe for Clyde and his staffers).

Establishing a government solution to a problem generally ensures that the problem will never be solved because the incentive for the bureaucrats is for it to endure forever. The problem is the reason they have a cushy job.

Some (but not enough) of the agencies created in the New Deal were eventually determined to be unconstitutional and were shut down. Others have become entrenched in our society and have spread to enormous proportions. Probably the most recognizable example is the Social Security Administration.

SOCIAL SECURITY ADMINISTRATION

Originally established with the purpose of providing a self-sustaining retirement insurance program to help prevent the elderly from living in poverty, the program has spread its tentacles into every American's life and is one of several federal programs that threaten to consume our entire economy. At the time of its inception it was projected and promised that only a very small portion of workers' earnings would be required to be contributed and that only a very small portion of our population would be receiving benefits at any given time. With benefits starting at age 65 and the average life expectancy only 58 for men and 62 for women in the early 1930's, an actuary using those figures would project that the program should never run out of money. Those average lifespans, however, are misleading because they factor in the then-current high death rate for infants and young children, who would never have contributed into the system nor received benefits. A more relevant statistic would be the number of Americans who are 65 or older and thus eligible to receive old age benefits.

SSA is the largest bureaucratic agency in the world

ELIGIBLE POPULATION FOR BENEFITS

Year	65-and-older Population
1930	6.7 million
1940	9.0 million
1950	12.7 million
1960	17.2 million
1970	20.9 million
1980	26.1 million
1990	31.9 million

Year	65-and-older Population
2000	34.9 million
2004	36.3 million
2050	86.7 million (projected)

The above data and projection is from the Administration on Aging, U.S. Dept. of Health and Human Services, and the US Bureau of the Census.

While it was originally promised that the contributions would never exceed one-percent (1%) of earnings, today seventy-five percent of workers pay more in FICA ("Federal Insurance Contributions Act," or "Social Security") contributions than they do in income taxes. When Medicare contributions are added in, the total contribution from worker and employer (or from self-employed worker) is over fifteen-percent (15%) of gross wages. The total revenue to the federal government from these contributions is approximately equivalent to what is received from individual income taxes for all workers. With this much income, we might expect that the system ought to be self-sustaining indefinitely.

> The Social Security Administration is technically not under the control of the Executive Branch, nor is it under the control of any other. It is what is called an Independent Agency; but it is headed by a Commissioner who is appointed by the President. Some Independent Agencies are run by boards of directors, others by commissions, the members of which are also appointed by the President. Congress has virtually no control over Independent Agencies and the President has not much more beyond making the appointments when a seat is vacated.

Perhaps it might be self-sustaining if it were not for the expansion of the program to include disability benefits for workers of any age who claim some form of disability. Today over eleven million Americans claim disability (and many may not have paid much if anything into the system, may not be actually disabled, and may not even be citizens). This drains approximately $100-150 billion per year from the coffers. There is no question that fraudulent claims are rampant; but we see no real effort to rein them in. Why? Because the more people enrolled into the system, the more powerful becomes the agency and, thus, the federal government. The motivation to grow and expand is much stronger than the motivation to stop the fraud. Power corrupts at the personal level and corrupts just as thoroughly at the organizational level. Thus, *the agency itself is complicit in the fraud.*

Social Security is a very delicate topic for any politician to discuss because so huge a portion of our society is now dependent upon it for some or all of their income. It is the granddaddy of all federal agencies because of its huge "success." Success not in providing value to American citizens, success in expanding itself and weaving itself inextricably into the fabric of America. It is the largest government program in the world. In FY2011 it paid out nearly $600 billion to about 45.5 million recipients, including retirees, dependents, and survivors.

Was it a noble idea to prevent poverty among the elderly? Certainly! But the establishment of this agency was probably not the best way to address that problem. The costs in dollars are staggering and may be enough to bankrupt our economy; but there are other costs as well.

- the ever-increasing contribution requirements are a disincentive to employers to hire Americans, thus encouraging outsourcing to other countries
- those same contribution requirements are a disincentive to workers to earn "earned income" encouraging "under-the-table" compensation
- the expanding costs pit one generation against another, creating classes of contributors and beneficiaries
- poor screening of applicants for disability payments encourages workers to become "disabled"
- dependency on Social Security gives politicians and government control over citizens behavior, especially voting behavior

- expectation of government taking care of us discourages thrift and prudent planning for retirement years

- money paid into the system rightfully belongs to the workers who paid it in; but it is being used to pay benefits to millions of people who did not pay into the system

- workers who paid into the system could have gotten a better return for their investment; but because of non-contributing recipients, are at risk of losing their investment in a system that may become bankrupt

- focusing so much power into a government agency inevitably leads to corruption and misuse of contributors' funds for political purposes

"If we can prevent the government from wasting the labors of the people, under the pretence of taking care of them, they must become happy." – Thomas Jefferson

In short, The Social Security Administration is a great example of a cure that is worse than the disease. A retirement insurance or pension program as it would have been administered by a private insurance or financial company would likely have provided better benefits and lower cost and would have been self-sustaining because it would have been profitable.

In 1980 Chile recognized all these same problems with their version of our Social Security system and took the radical step of dismantling the government-run system in favor of a private-sector solution of Pension Savings Accounts. The result is that benefits to retired workers, disabled, and dependents are 50-100% higher and, with the adverse incentives that a government system engenders removed, the unemployment rate dropped 5%, and the savings rate of their citizens increased sharply. This, of course, does not even mention that the financial solvency of their government was secured.

The most important question we must ask, though, is: how did the federal government acquire the power to establish such an agency in the first place? By what authority was it done?

8. Spawning Agencies

The names of agencies are often deceptive. They are not even always called an "agency." Many of them are called a "program," an "office," or something else. The government's own definition of an agency, from the Administrative Procedures Act of 1946, describes any government unit with the power to determine private rights and obligations by rulemaking or adjudication. To demonstrate how efficient our government is at spawning new agencies, below is a list of new agencies created in a single stroke by the Affordable Healthcare Act ("Obamacare"). This list was originally published by Glenn Beck on one of his broadcasts to illustrate how explosively our government can expand. Every one of these new entities has the power, or the potential power, to issue rules or regulations that would have a profound impact upon our lives.

NEW OBAMACARE AGENCIES

1. Grant program for consumer assistance offices (Section 1002, p. 37)
2. Grant program for states to monitor premium increases (Section 1003, p. 42)
3. Committee to review administrative simplification standards (Section 1104, p. 71)
4. Demonstration program for state wellness programs (Section 1201, p. 93)
5. Grant program to establish state Exchanges (Section 1311(a), p. 130)
6. State American Health Benefit Exchanges (Section 1311(b), p. 131)
7. Exchange grants to establish consumer navigator programs (Section 1311(i), p. 150)
8. Grant program for state cooperatives (Section 1322, p. 169)
9. Advisory board for state cooperatives (Section 1322(b)(3), p. 173)
10. Private purchasing council for state cooperatives (Section 1322(d), p. 177)
11. State basic health plan programs (Section 1331, p. 201)
12. State-based reinsurance program (Section 1341, p. 226)
13. Program of risk corridors for individual and small group markets (Section 1342, p. 233)
14. Program to determine eligibility for Exchange participation (Section 1411, p. 267)
15. Program for advance determination of tax credit eligibility (Section 1412, p. 288)
16. Grant program to implement health IT enrollment standards (Section 1561, p. 370)
17. Federal Coordinated Health Care Office for dual eligible beneficiaries (Section 2602, p. 512)
18. Medicaid quality measurement program (Section 2701, p. 518)
19. Medicaid health home program for people with chronic conditions, and grants for planning same (Sec. 2703, p. 524)

20. Medicaid demonstration project to evaluate bundled payments (Section 2704, p. 532)
21. Medicaid demonstration project for global payment system (Section 2705, p. 536)
22. Medicaid demonstration project for accountable care organizations (Section 2706, p. 538)
23. Medicaid demonstration project for emergency psychiatric care (Section 2707, p. 540)
24. Grant program for delivery of services to individuals with postpartum depression (Section 2952(b), p. 591)
25. State allotments for grants to promote personal responsibility education programs (Section 2953, p. 596)
26. Medicare value-based purchasing program (Section 3001(a), p. 613)
27. Medicare value-based purchasing demonstration program for critical access hospitals (Section 3001(b), p. 637)
28. Medicare value-based purchasing program for skilled nursing facilities (Section 3006(a), p. 666)
29. Medicare value-based purchasing program for home health agencies (Section 3006(b), p. 668)
30. Interagency Working Group on Health Care Quality (Section 3012, p. 688)
31. Grant program to develop health care quality measures (Section 3013, p. 693)
32. Center for Medicare and Medicaid Innovation (Section 3021, p. 712)
33. Medicare shared savings program (Section 3022, p. 728)
34. Medicare pilot program on payment bundling (Section 3023, p. 739)
35. Independence at home medical practice demonstration program (Section 3024, p. 752)
36. Program for use of patient safety organizations to reduce hospital readmission rates (Section 3025(b), p. 775)
37. Community-based care transitions program (Section 3026, p. 776)
38. Demonstration project for payment of complex diagnostic laboratory tests (Section 3113, p. 800)
39. Medicare hospice concurrent care demonstration project (Section 3140, p. 850)
40. Independent Payment Advisory Board (Section 3403, p. 982)
41. Consumer Advisory Council for Independent Payment Advisory Board (Section 3403, p. 1027)
42. Grant program for technical assistance to providers implementing health quality practices (Section 3501, p. 1043)
43. Grant program to establish interdisciplinary health teams (Section 3502, p. 1048)
44. Grant program to implement medication therapy management (Section 3503, p. 1055)
45. Grant program to support emergency care pilot programs (Section 3504, p. 1061)
46. Grant program to promote universal access to trauma services (Section 3505(b), p. 1081)
47. Grant program to develop and promote shared decision-making aids (Section 3506, p. 1088)
48. Grant program to support implementation of shared decision-making (Section 3506, p. 1091)
49. Grant program to integrate quality improvement in clinical education (Section 3508, p. 1095)
50. Health and Human Services Coordinating Committee on Women?s Health (Section 3509(a), p. 1098)

51. Centers for Disease Control Office of Women?s Health (Section 3509(b), p. 1102)
52. Agency for Healthcare Research and Quality Office of Women?s Health (Section 3509(e), p. 1105)
53. Health Resources and Services Administration Office of Women?s Health (Section 3509(f), p. 1106)
54. Food and Drug Administration Office of Women's Health (Section 3509(g), p. 1109)
55. National Prevention, Health Promotion, and Public Health Council (Section 4001, p. 1114)
56. Advisory Group on Prevention, Health Promotion, and Integrative and Public Health (Section 4001(f), p. 1117)
57. Prevention and Public Health Fund (Section 4002, p. 1121)
58. Community Preventive Services Task Force (Section 4003(b), p. 1126)
59. Grant program to support school-based health centers (Section 4101, p. 1135)
60. Grant program to promote research-based dental caries disease management (Section 4102, p. 1147)
61. Grant program for States to prevent chronic disease in Medicaid beneficiaries (Section 4108, p. 1174)
62. Community transformation grants (Section 4201, p. 1182)
63. Grant program to provide public health interventions (Section 4202, p. 1188)
64. Demonstration program of grants to improve child immunization rates (Section 4204(b), p. 1200)
65. Pilot program for risk-factor assessments provided through community health centers (Section 4206, p. 1215)
66. Grant program to increase epidemiology and laboratory capacity (Section 4304, p. 1233)
67. Interagency Pain Research Coordinating Committee (Section 4305, p. 1238)
68. National Health Care Workforce Commission (Section 5101, p. 1256)
69. Grant program to plan health care workforce development activities (Section 5102(c), p. 1275)
70. Grant program to implement health care workforce development activities (Section 5102(d), p. 1279)
71. Pediatric specialty loan repayment program (Section 5203, p. 1295)
72. Public Health Workforce Loan Repayment Program (Section 5204, p. 1300)
73. Allied Health Loan Forgiveness Program (Section 5205, p. 1305)
74. Grant program to provide mid-career training for health professionals (Section 5206, p. 1307)
75. Grant program to fund nurse-managed health clinics (Section 5208, p. 1310)
76. Grant program to support primary care training programs (Section 5301, p. 1315)
77. Grant program to fund training for direct care workers (Section 5302, p. 1322)
78. Grant program to develop dental training programs (Section 5303, p. 1325)
79. Demonstration program to increase access to dental health care in underserved communities (Sec. 5304, p. 1331)
80. Grant program to promote geriatric education centers (Section 5305, p. 1334)
81. Grant program to promote health professionals entering geriatrics

(Section 5305, p. 1339)

82. Grant program to promote training in mental and behavioral health (Section 5306, p. 1344)

83. Grant program to promote nurse retention programs (Section 5309, p. 1354)

84. Student loan forgiveness for nursing school faculty (Section 5311(b), p. 1360)

85. Grant program to promote positive health behaviors and outcomes (Section 5313, p. 1364)

86. Public Health Sciences Track for medical students (Section 5315, p. 1372)

87. Primary Care Extension Program to educate providers (Section 5405, p. 1404)

88. Grant program for demonstration projects to address health workforce shortage needs (Section 5507, p. 1442)

89. Grant program for demonstration projects to develop training programs for home health aides (Sec. 5507, p. 1447)

90. Grant program to establish new primary care residency programs (Section 5508(a), p. 1458)

91. Program of payments to teaching health centers that sponsor medical residency training (Section 5508(c), p. 1462)

92. Graduate nurse education demonstration program (Section 5509, p. 1472)

93. Grant program to establish demonstration projects for community-based mental health settings (Sec. 5604, p. 1486)

94. Commission on Key National Indicators (Section 5605, p. 1489)

95. Quality assurance and performance improvement program for skilled nursing facilities (Section 6102, p. 1554)

96. Special focus facility program for skilled nursing facilities (Section 6103(a)(3), p. 1561)

97. Special focus facility program for nursing facilities (Section 6103(b)(3), p. 1568)

98. National independent monitor pilot program for skilled nursing facilities and nursing facilities (Section 6112, p. 1589)

99. Demonstration projects for nursing facilities involved in the culture change movement (Section 6114, p. 1597)

100. Patient-Centered Outcomes Research Institute (Section 6301, p. 1619)

101. Standing methodology committee for Patient-Centered Outcomes Research Institute (Section 6301, p. 1629)

102. Board of Governors for Patient-Centered Outcomes Research Institute (Section 6301, p. 1638)

103. Patient-Centered Outcomes Research Trust Fund (Section 6301(e), p. 1656)

104. Elder Justice Coordinating Council (Section 6703, p. 1773)

105. Advisory Board on Elder Abuse, Neglect, and Exploitation (Section 6703, p. 1776)

106. Grant program to create elder abuse forensic centers (Section 6703, p. 1783)

107. Grant program to promote continuing education for long-term care staffers (Section 6703, p. 1787)

108. Grant program to improve management practices and training (Section 6703, p. 1788)

109. Grant program to subsidize costs of electronic health records (Section 6703, p. 1791)

110. Grant program to promote adult protective services (Section 6703, p.

1796)
111. Grant program to conduct elder abuse detection and prevention (Section 6703, p. 1798)
112. Grant program to support long-term care ombudsmen (Section 6703, p. 1800)
113. National Training Institute for long-term care surveyors (Section 6703, p. 1806)
114. Grant program to fund State surveys of long-term care residences (Section 6703, p. 1809)
115. CLASS Independence Fund (Section 8002, p. 1926)
116. CLASS Independence Fund Board of Trustees (Section 8002, p. 1927)
117. CLASS Independence Advisory Council (Section 8002, p. 1931)
118. Personal Care Attendants Workforce Advisory Panel (Section 8002(c), p. 1938)
119. Multi-state health plans offered by Office of Personnel Management (Section 10104(p), p. 2086)
120. Advisory board for multi-state health plans (Section 10104(p), p. 2094)
121. Pregnancy Assistance Fund (Section 10212, p. 2164)
122. Value-based purchasing program for ambulatory surgical centers (Section 10301, p. 2176)
123. Demonstration project for payment adjustments to home health services (Section 10315, p. 2200)
124. Pilot program for care of individuals in environmental emergency declaration areas (Section 10323, p. 2223)
125. Grant program to screen at-risk individuals for environmental health conditions (Section 10323(b), p. 2231)
126. Pilot programs to implement value-based purchasing (Section 10326, p. 2242)
127. Grant program to support community-based collaborative care networks (Section 10333, p. 2265)
128. Centers for Disease Control Office of Minority Health (Section 10334, p. 2272)
129. Health Resources and Services Administration Office of Minority Health (Section 10334, p. 2272)
130. Substance Abuse and Mental Health Services Administration Office of Minority Health (Section 10334, p. 2272)
131. Agency for Healthcare Research and Quality Office of Minority Health (Section 10334, p. 2272)
132. Food and Drug Administration Office of Minority Health (Section 10334, p. 2272)
133. Centers for Medicare and Medicaid Services Office of Minority Health (Section 10334, p. 2272)
134. Grant program to promote small business wellness programs (Section 10408, p. 2285)
135. Cures Acceleration Network (Section 10409, p. 2289)
136. Cures Acceleration Network Review Board (Section 10409, p. 2291)
137. Grant program for Cures Acceleration Network (Section 10409, p. 2297)
138. Grant program to promote centers of excellence for depression (Section 10410, p. 2304)
139. Advisory committee for young women?s breast health awareness education campaign (Section 10413, p. 2322)
140. Grant program to provide assistance to provide information to young women with breast cancer (Sec. 10413, p. 2326)

141. Interagency Access to Health Care in Alaska Task Force (Section 10501, p. 2329)
142. Grant program to train nurse practitioners as primary care providers (Section 10501(e), p. 2332)
143. Grant program for community-based diabetes prevention (Section 10501(g), p. 2337)
144. Grant program for providers who treat a high percentage of medically underserved populations (Section 10501(k), p. 2343)
145. Grant program to recruit students to practice in underserved communities (Section 10501(l), p. 2344)
146. Community Health Center Fund (Section 10503, p. 2355)
147. Demonstration project to provide access to health care for the uninsured at reduced fees (Section 10504, p. 2357)
148. Demonstration program to explore alternatives to tort litigation (Section 10607, p. 2369)
149. Indian Health demonstration program for chronic shortages of health professionals (S. 1790, Section 112, p. 24)
150. Office of Indian Men?s Health (S. 1790, Section 136, p. 71)
151. Indian Country modular component facilities demonstration program (S. 1790, Section 146, p. 108)
152. Indian mobile health stations demonstration program (S. 1790, Section 147, p. 111)
153. Office of Direct Service Tribes (S. 1790, Section 172, p. 151)
154. Indian Health Service mental health technician training program (S. 1790, Section 181, p. 173)
155. Indian Health Service program for treatment of child sexual abuse victims (S. 1790, Section 181, p. 192)
156. Indian Health Service program for treatment of domestic violence and sexual abuse (S. 1790, Section 181, p. 194)
157. Indian youth elemental health demonstration project (S. 1790, Section 181, p. 204)
158. Indian youth life skills demonstration project (S. 1790, Section 181, p. 220)
159. Indian Health Service Director of HIV/AIDS Prevention and Treatment (S. 1790, Section 199B, p. 258)

Recently, the Supreme Court upheld the constitutionality of most of the controversial Healthcare Act even though many of the parts that were upheld appear to be clearly unconstitutional to us, and to numerous constitutional scholars, and in spite of the fact that the majority of Americans oppose it. This is reminiscent of the Court's upholding other clearly unconstitutional acts during the New Deal. Back then, Roosevelt had threatened to "pack the courts" with judges and justices sympathetic to his expansionist ambitions if the Court did not acquiesce. He thus managed to intimidate them into aiding and abetting him. We can only speculate as to how our current President managed a similar feat. In both instances, it is obvious that the Supreme Court, which is supposed to be insulated from political pressure because of their lifetime appointments, succumbed to such pressure and abandoned their fundamental responsibility to defend our Constitution.

A NEW KIND OF TAX

The power to tax is the power to destroy. – John Marshall

In order to rationalize the ruling to uphold the "individual mandate" to purchase health insurance that is approved by the government and the penalty on citizens for not complying, Justice Roberts, who initially opposed the new law, did a 180-degree turnaround and declared that the penalty was in fact a *tax*. Of course, the President and the leadership of the Congress assured us that it was definitely *not* a tax when they were promoting the bill; but now it seems to have morphed into a tax.

Since it will be the Bureaucracy that will determine whether your health care insurance is acceptable or not, and it is the Bureaucracy that will levy this new "tax" and decide how much it will be, and it is the Bureaucracy that will collect it with the full force of the federal government behind it, the Supreme Court has just expanded the powers of the Fourth Branch even further. Now, in addition to being empowered to make de-facto law and enforce it, it is empowered to levy taxes.

> The Constitution clearly states that all revenue bills (taxes) must be initiated by the House of Representatives in Article I, Section 7. The next section (Enumerated Powers) states that Congress shall have the power to lay and collect taxes. That means *only* Congress.

Remember, this Bureaucracy is almost entirely in service to the Executive Branch—the President. Our Constitution clearly grants the right to tax exclusively to Congress. More specifically, revenue bills must start in the House of Representatives and then be approved by the Senate (which may propose amendments). This new-found administrative taxing authority completely sidesteps the Constitution and gives taxing powers to the Executive Branch through its Bureaucracy.

Do you believe that this will go unnoticed by the Statists in either major political party? Do you think they will *not* find more new ways to levy taxes without the bother of going through Congress? I believe that the only real question is: how long will it take before they do.

When you compare the achievements of FDR at going around the Constitution versus those of our current administration, you can only conclude that our government has gotten better – better at nullifying our liberties!

CELL PHONE WELFARE

Another good example of how Administrative Law has enabled federal agencies to extract money from you to be used for things you probably do not support is found in the Federal Communications Commission. This agency was formed in 1934 by an act of Congress and has grown exponentially every decade since. The original charter of the FCC was to regulate the airwaves accessible by the public, mostly via the AM radio band.

Over the years the agency has been expanded numerous times to regulate everything from cable TV to satellite radio. If you look at your telephone, cable, cell phone and

The Federal Communications Commission now wants to tax your internet access

satellite bill, you will see the footprints of the Bureaucracy every month. Comcast, one of the nation's largest providers of cable and internet communications, lists no less than 11 fees, charges and taxes authorized or collected by the FCC on their web page that explains your bill. Some of these charges are listed as state or local, others are directly attributed to the federal government.

Did you know that when you pay your own bills for cable, cell phone, telephone, or internet you are also paying someone else's bills? There is a charge on every bill called "Universal Service Charge," which is collected and applied to the "Universal Service Fund." This fund is managed by a government-sanctioned monopoly called the Universal Service Administrative Company, or USAC. I bet you've never heard of them. The USAC is a non-profit company, designated by the FCC to manage the Universal Service Fund.

One of the main uses of the Universal Service Fund is to assist low-income families with access to communications - a sort of welfare for phone and cable access if you will.

Who monitors this $30 billion fund? Who does the hiring and firing at USAC? Who provides the oversight for their programs? Why is a private company given a monopoly to spend taxes being collected through an appointed commission?

Most Americans have no issue with helping the needy or those going through a bad time. I happen to be one of them. What I do have an issue with is money being collected without elected representation, money being distributed without elected representation and the lack of oversight from elected representation.

This gets worse the further you dig into it. The amount collected monthly from your bill isn't a set amount. The USAC determines which programs, needs, and expenditures it is going to support and then goes back to let the FCC know how much money it wants. There is no budget, no reconciliation, and no limit on what you may be charged.

> The FCC, through a vehicle it has created called the *Connect America Fund*, it now attempting to also begin taxing internet service, once again bypassing Congressional involvement.

Can you imagine running your household like this? You determine how much money you want for the month, and go demand it of your employer. Now that's the type of job I want!

There is little public information available on the USAC. The average citizen can't do an internet search and find out how many employees there are, average salaries, monthly expenditures, or even how much the person running the operation is paid. We, as citizens supporting this organization, have no clue how they are spending our money. Given the recent news reports of lavish Las Vegas conferences, outrageous luxury during offsite meetings, and general waste by several government agencies, it's not difficult to imagine some of the $30 billion being misappropriated. Is most of the money going to administration costs like in our welfare system?

> I can not find in the Constitution the provision that gives citizens the *right* to cable TV or a cell phone.

In addition the FCC forces, through regulation, private companies to broadcast public service announcements through the Public Broadcasting Network? On the surface, many people would consider this a virtue of the FCC.

What most people don't realize is that the provider can charge you, the customer, for this service. Often called a "pass-through" fee, the FCC's rules about how much the provider can bill you are loosely defined at best.

You, the consumer, are being forced to buy a product for an indeterminate price. The mandatory enrollment in the Affordable Healthcare Act received a lot of attention in the press over something similar. In reality, the federal government, through its Bureaucracy, has been forcing us to purchase a lot of things for many years.

No Place to Go

In "The Road to Serfdom," Friedrich A. Hayek describes how in Hitler's Germany the government did not have to *own* the means of production because it could regulate it to the point at which the natural Capitalist motivators of profit or customer satisfaction were subordinated to compliance with an endless chain of rules and mandates handed down from government bureaucrats. Thus, using regulatory control, not ownership, of about 53% of German industry, the government had sufficient leverage to be able to control the entire economy making all German citizens dependent upon their rulers.

With government expenditures at all levels now totaling about forty percent (40%) of our national income and a Federal Register containing over 73,000 pages of regulations, we can see that America is already alarmingly close to a tipping point from which there is no return.

Note: Germany reached that point of no return and, had it not been for the intervention of the USA, would be virtually a slave state today with Hitler's successors as their eternal ruling class. When America passes that point, who will come to our rescue? The Statists will have captured the ultimate prize and the World will enter a new Dark Age of hopeless subservience to tyranny. With the power of the United States neutralized no nation on Earth will be able to resist domination.

We often hear political candidates promise to fight against government regulations. Some even promise to fight to abolish certain government agencies. But if the government can create agencies as easily as we have shown here, we must concede that it can certainly give birth to new ones faster than we can shut them down. In the Introduction I showed that to fight against one regulation at a time was not a strategy that could win. Now we should be able to see that to stop the runaway expansion of government will require a more effective strategy than to even fight agency by agency. We must aim still higher. We must aim at the real source of their power, **Administrative Law**. For example, proper reform would render the entire Affordable Healthcare Act toothless since all of its harm is done through federal agencies acting outside the Enumerated Powers.

Rafael Cruz is a fiercely patriotic American citizen with the courage to speak loudly and clearly about the state our nation is in. Rafael was not born in the US. He immigrated to the US from Cuba to escape the tyranny wrought by Fidel Castro, a charismatic man who concealed the fact that he was a Communist until after he had established himself in power. As an idealistic teenager, Rafael had been swayed by Castro's promises and fought in the revolution to overthrow Batista and to put Castro in power. Then, the new Communist regime revealed its true colors and seized all of young Rafael's family's assets, including their home, food, and clothes leaving them to die of starvation. Massive oppression of the people led to conditions even worse than they had been under the dictator Batista.

Your author with Ted and Rafael Cruz on the campaign trail. Ted's campaign went better than my own and he is our new Senator from Texas.

Rafael speaks often to audiences of every size about what he saw in Cuba and what he sees now in America. He taught his son, Ted Cruz, American values and a love for this country and our Constitution from the time Ted was old enough to speak. At eleven years of age, Ted and some friends traveled to schools giving a lecture on the Constitution and reciting it from memory. Ted is now the presumptive next new US Senator from Texas.

Both of the Cruz's have a thorough understanding of the importance of standing up to save our way of life before it is too late. Sadly, many of us born into this land of liberty take it all for granted. We like to enjoy the fruits of freedom; but are not anxious to pay the price.

> "The tree of liberty must be refreshed from time to time, with the blood of patriots and tyrants" – Thomas Jefferson

It is my hope that instead of the blood that Jefferson spoke of, we will be able to purchase our continued liberty with a little of our time, some hard work, and a dose of courage.

When he speaks publicly, Rafael Cruz usually makes it a point to say: "When Cuba fell to tyranny, thank God I had the United States to flee to. When the United States falls, there will be no place left to go."

9. The Real Price of Depression and War

Nobody can deny that The Great Depression, and World War II, which followed it, had huge costs to most Americans. The costs can be measured in lives lost and wealth destroyed; but there is another cost that too few people ever consider: liberty lost.

> *"He has erected a multitude of New Offices, and sent hither swarms of Officers to harrass our people, and eat out their substance." – Declaration of Independence*

Memorial statue of Franklin Delano Roosevelt

It is said that extreme cases result in bad law. That is true at every level. The fear and panic of the Great Depression, and then the crisis of the war that followed gave government the opportunity to take huge leaps forward in its efforts to expand. The most notable action was that of FDR in establishing federal regulatory agencies to supposedly correct the flaws in our capitalist economic system that allegedly allowed the huge depression to occur. FDR established a laundry list of new federal agencies to regulate everything from farming to housing to jobs to banking in the name of the public good. Later, the war gave an inarguable reason to create even more federal departments with vast regulatory powers. Many of these agencies exist to this day and possess powers amplified many times beyond what they originally had. In his classic novel, "1984," George Orwell illustrates how war gives governments the perfect excuse to assume dictatorial powers. I am sure that his observations of the expansion of power in many countries on both sides during WWII had a huge impact on his thinking.

Statism: In this book you will notice from time to time I will use the term "statist" or "statism." I wish to be clear as to what I mean by that.

We often hear about political dichotomies between opposing philosophies, such as Left versus Right, Communism versus Capitalism, and so forth. I believe that these terms describe battles in a larger war between the opposing philosophies of Statism versus Populism. Statism holds that power should be centered in government (The State) while Populism holds that power should be centered in the People. There are many political systems that can be classified as statist: Communist, Socialist, Fascist, Monarchist, and others. There are two that can be classified as populist: Democratic and Republican (not referring to the two major political parties in the US that have names based on these forms of government). Our Founders clearly intended to establish a constitutional representative republic. Proponents of a more expansive central government are clearly statist-leaning in their philosophies. Proponents of a more limited central government, like myself, are clearly populist-leaning.

But how could the federal government, which consisted of its three branches, each with specifically limited powers, have stuck its fingers into so many aspects of our private lives? According to the Constitution, it could not! So, FDR used his immense popularity as the perceived saviour of our economy to coerce a compliant Legislature to enact laws, called Administrative Laws that empowered these agencies with administrative powers to make and enforce rules and regulations.

The power to enforce includes the ability to levy fines, to confiscate property, and to imprison offenders. That gives these rules and regulations the force of law, even though they are not laws per se.

- They have never been voted on.

- They do not pass the scrutiny that a law would have to pass.

- They do not confine themselves to the constitutional limits on the federal government, even though the agencies are a part of the federal government.

It should be noted that frustration over the current issue of Affordable Healthcare Act (Obamacare) is fueled by the many abhorrent features of its implementation. Then it should be noted that every one of them is implemented by agencies created by the Act or tasked by the Act to perform functions offensive to us, such as the so-called "death panels," the "individual mandate," "healthcare rationing," and many others. The Obamacare issue is actually a manifestation of the Administrative Law issue.

The desperation and fear that Americans felt at the time of the Great Depression led them to surrender huge portions of their liberty to a charismatic personality who promised to deliver them from despair. Much the same happened in Germany, since the German economy was strongly linked to the US economy, at about that same time, by the way. Adolf Hitler used the economic crisis as a justification to grab regulatory control, not ownership, of key parts of the German economy and industry. That led to absolute control over all of Germany and its people.

In America, the implementation of these Administrative Laws empowering an extra-Constitutional bureaucracy created what is for all intents and purposes a **Fourth Branch** of our federal government—one that is not hindered by any checks and balances or even by the Constitution's limits on the powers of the federal government.

CIRCUMVENTING THE CONSTITUTION

Evidence that this unsanctioned Fourth Branch was designed to, and is used to step around Constitutional restrictions on the powers of the federal government is found everywhere; but perhaps it is never more blatantly apparent than in the recent use of EPA (Environmental Protection Agency) regulating powers to do what our elected representatives voted *not* to do.

When Congress did not pass new laws that were promoted by the President (Obama) putting caps on the production of CO_2 (carbon dioxide), the President merely did an end-run around Congress by directing a federal agency, EPA, to accomplish exactly what Congress had declined to do. They did it by initiating rules and regulations which are as potent and effective as laws. This has the effect of completely disenfranchising our elected representatives in both the House

48

of Representatives and Senate, and therefore all citizens of the United States in favor of the vote of a single person, the President. All of the checks and balances that are supposed to prevent a rogue President from ruling by command have been bypassed. Our representation and that of the 50 States in our federal government has now been nullified.

CURE WORSE THAN DISEASE

An example of how the extreme circumstances in the Depression Era resulted in a solution that has long outlived its usefulness and lives on and on is the Farm Bill, which is renewed and adjusted (usually upward) every five years.

It may have been justified in 1933 to protect the producers of our food from going out of business; but in today's very different agricultural environment, it wastes hundreds of billions of dollars subsidizing giant farm corporations (not the small farmers it was advertised to help), often for *not* producing crops in order to keep prices higher. This hurts us in several ways. It reduces the production of some foods and increases our costs at the grocery store while costing us tax dollars. It also artificially creates a demand and thus increases production of other crops causing an excess of them, distorting markets both domestically and in other countries.

The concept of central planning has been shown to not work over and over throughout history. The marketplace provides a truer picture of demand so that producers can adjust production accordingly. Farm Subsidies, America's largest corporate welfare program, are an all-around losing arrangement for America; but politicians do not have the backbone to shut it down.

Farming is certainly a very important industry in America and we do not want to see farmers put out of business by transient fluctuations in prices or markets; but there are many non-government methods for controlling risk, such as: insurance, hedging, and by simply diversifying their crops.

Additionally, a host of non-farm-related programs sprouted from the Department of Agriculture (USDA), most notably the Food Stamp program (now called SNAP). This program takes taxpayer dollars and subsidizes a rapidly growing segment of our population, making them dependent

Not surprisingly, the Food Stamp program invites fraud.

on government and therefore more easily manipulated and controlled. At the time of this writing over fifteen percent (15%+) of Americans are receiving Food Stamps and the number is growing daily as our government actually solicits for more enrollees. The US Department of Agriculture proclaims its goal to "increase participation in the Supplemental Nutrition Assistance Program" (SNAP) on its "Outreach Toolkits" webpage. As if that alone was not a sufficient corruption of the Department of Agriculture, it is now running Spanish-only ads (including ads run in Mexico!) to solicit greater participation in the program by illegal aliens.

Aside: Because of an unusual provision in our tax code, the Additional Child Tax Credit, illegal aliens will also receive over $7 billion in tax credits for children who do not even live in the US.

It should be noted that at the time of this writing conservative members of the House of Representatives are trying to pass a Farm Bill that includes a major downsizing. I hope they are successful; but that will only be a temporary and partial correction – a band-aid on a gaping wound. Even if this Congress succeeds, a future Congress will be subjected to pressure to re-expand it and will likely succumb.

What started as a seemingly beneficial, short-term government solution to a perceived problem has grown into a malignant disease more dangerous than the original problem. Heritage Foundation is currently doing investigative reporting on profligate waste in USDA, including, for example, the hiring of one single intern at a cost of $2 million.

*"Don't apply a permanent solution to a temporary problem."
This is advice given to people considering suicide; but I believe
it applies aptly to many government regulations as well.
Ironically, some people might contend that America is
committing "suicide by regulation."*

A REMEDY IS NEEDED

Clearly this Fourth Branch of our government must be brought
under control and fit into a framework that makes it answerable
to the People and to the States. The solution must be structural
and not one that relies on always having conservative control of
the White House, the Senate, and the House of Representatives.
In fact, you will see later in this book that even having
conservative control of our federal government does not fix the
problem.

*"Government is not the solution to our problem. Government
is the problem." — Ronald Reagan*

The Founders understood that human beings were subject to
human nature and were fallible. They tried to architect a
structure of government that pitted opposing forces against one
another to suppress the ambitions of all government offices.
They knew that from time to time we would elect officeholders
who were less than the best and designed a system that would
be resilient to the attempts to amass power by ambitious
officials, whether elected or appointed.

> Legislative "gridlock," which is much maligned today, was actually built
> into our system by design. The Founders did not want laws to be
> added haphazardly or without thorough vetting.

The Fourth Branch must be subjected to checks and balances
similar to those that restrict the three constitutionally
sanctioned branches of our government.

Some may believe that the federal government acts as it does out of genuine concern for our welfare, albeit misguided, uninformed concern. While I was working to help a friend run for Congress in the mid-90's, I had occasion to meet Dick Armey, the conservative Texas Member of the House who was Minority Leader, soon to become Majority Leader. Armey, a former economics professor, said that before he went to Congress he believed that the folks in Washington did not understand how bad their policies were and needed some education. By the end of his first 2-year term his eyes had been opened to the fact that they knew *exactly* what they were doing and how damaging it was—*that was their intention!*

10. Creating an Oligarchy

Many Americans observe the actions of the government in such programs as the Welfare System and see that it is behaving in a *Socialist* manner. Other Americans see the government imposing regulations to control business and industry (the means of production) and see that as *Fascist* behavior. The Left in America tends to portray Fascism as evil, citing Adolf Hitler or Mussolini; and Socialism as benevolent. As a result, in many people's minds, Socialism and Fascism are polar opposites. That is an entirely false image. It is an intentional misconception fostered by those who wish to have the argument that since Fascism is so bad, its opposite, Socialism, must be good.

In truth, Socialism and Fascism are barely distinguishable from one another. That is also true for all of Socialism's alter egos: Communism, Marxism, et cetera; and for Fascism's alter ego, Progressivism. They are all similar because they all involve concentration of power into the state (Statism) as opposed to in the citizenry ("the consent of the governed," as our Founders put it). They all establish a ruling class of people who govern over the masses. It does not matter what they call themselves, in the end they all behave more-or-less the same. Remember, power corrupts!

In fact, any structure of governance that establishes a ruling class is called an "oligarchy" regardless what distinguishes the classes. It could be an economic separation in which the rich aristocracy rules over the commoners. It could be a Communist structure in which the Nomenklatura rules over the citizens. It could be a Royal Family and their court, such as in classic Monarchy. It could be a religious hierarchy, as found in the Middle East, or a caste system as in India and other countries. Even a dictatorship is really an oligarchy because no single individual can maintain power without a coterie of supporters who benefit from their positions. Regardless what the outward image may be, under the surface there is a privileged group of people who hold power over the much larger mass of common people.

Inevitably, the ruling class will take greater and greater advantage of their position of power and the circumstance of the common people will deteriorate. The attitude of the rulers *always* evolves (degenerates?) into the belief that the masses exist to serve them, the Ruling Class.

"The price of liberty is eternal vigilance." – Patrick Henry

Throughout the history of mankind, oligarchy is by far the most frequently occurring form of government. We Americans have lived sheltered lives in that respect. We tend to believe that power actually resides with the People and that, in the end, the will of the people will naturally always win out. In fact, that is only true if the People continuously remain vigilant and defend their rights against a constant pressure to erode them in favor of state powers and establishment of a privileged ruling class. We, as citizens of a free society that values individual rights, constitute only a tiny fraction of a percent of all the humans who have occupied the Earth throughout history. A society based on individual freedom is an aberration in the course of world history—a new paradigm—an experiment established by our Founding Fathers in hopes that we would have the wisdom and courage to preserve such a radical departure from the historical norm.

The Myth of a Benevolent Dictatorship: To anyone who studies forms of government, it soon becomes apparent that there is no perfect form. Every scheme has its flaws. That leads many to believe that the best form of government would be a benevolent dictatorship, rule by an absolute monarch who somehow retained the best interests of the common people as his/her foremost consideration. There may have been a few such rulers in history (more likely, there were a few who managed to project the *image* that they were a benevolent dictator, though they really were not). But even if we accept the premise that a ruler might somehow manage to resist the corrupting effects of power, we must recognize that no such ruler is immortal and he will eventually be replaced by someone else. The person who succeeds him or her is not likely to share the same priorities as our benevolent king and the situation will soon degenerate into the classic oligarchy scenario—a ruling class governing with little regard for the will or needs of the common people.

So, is there a ruling class emerging in America now? I believe that there is! Of course, it does include hundreds, or thousands, of elected officials who enjoy all sorts of privileges and benefits of their offices; but it also includes millions of government employees (tens of millions if you include all levels of government) who are not elected; but enjoy immense benefits that we commoners do not enjoy — *but that we pay for.* The arrogance that is being demonstrated by many of these government apparatchiks is appalling. We recently saw a YouTube video produced by Government Services Administration (GSA) workers mocking taxpayers with "rap" lyrics bragging that they get paid exorbitant salaries, cannot be fired, and receive generous benefits that we have no choice but to pay for, regardless whether we are even able to support our own families.

Ruling classes everywhere eventually come to view the commoners with disdain. It is just human nature that they become accustomed to the perquisites and rationalize that it is right and proper for them to benefit as they do and that grumbling and complaining by the common class is merely a display of ingratitude. Sooner or later, that ingratitude becomes unlawful and a punishable offense.

It has long been against the law in the United States to threaten the life of the President. Most of us concede that it is reasonable for actual threats to be unlawful; but recently, our President has moved to make it unlawful to *criticize* him, or to *protest* against him (HR347, the "Criminalizing Protest Bill").

To be more accurate, I should say that we are evolving into a three-tiered class system with a Ruling Class, an Administrative Class, and a Common Class, the first two of which I sometimes group together and call the Privileged Classes.

The Ruling Class consists of high office holders, whether elected or appointed. Many, but not all, elected officials at this moment would be included (there are a few sincere patriots in office who understand and wish to fight against the problems we describe in this book). Most department heads and sub-heads at levels that can influence policy in federal agencies would be included.

The Administrative Class consists of most of the federal employees who are below the policy-making level; but enjoy the privilege of their positions at our expense. There are definitely some government employees who do not view their positions thusly; but every year that passes, the composition of the government workforce becomes more-and-more an entitled, privileged subculture of our society.

The Common Class, of course, is us—the vast majority of American citizens. We pay for all of the benefits that the above two classes enjoy and our needs and wishes are becoming progressively more subordinated to the priorities of the privileged classes. We are mocked by the privileged class members and manipulated by them, usually for their benefit, not ours. They maneuver to make us increasingly reliant upon them for basic needs so that we can be more easily controlled. They resist and thwart any efforts by us to be independent and self-sufficient.

> *"A taxpayer is someone who works for the government but doesn't have to take the civil service examination"* – Ronald Reagan

Later in this book you will see that this dependency is a strategy promoted by Joseph Stalin and embraced by Statist government officials everywhere.

CIVIL SERVICE UNIONS

Before I begin this discussion, I will state that I am neither pro-union, nor anti-union. I have seen both good and bad from labor unions; but I do believe that unionization of government workers is a serious problem. There is a fundamental difference between unionizing private-sector workers and unionizing government workers.

Suppose that the Johnson family started a business manufacturing jams and jellies from fruits they grew on their own farm. Imagine that their products became quite popular and eventually they started purchasing fruits from other farmers in order to produce more of their product, which they were now distributing nationwide from a plant that employed several hundred workers—workers who have just decided to unionize.

The workers negotiate with the Johnson's regarding their demands. The Johnson family must consider the demands of the workers and make counter offers to try to reach a compromise, or they could simply reject the demands and risk a strike that would shut down their operations. If they considered the demands to be unreasonable, they might even decide to shut down operations themselves and shut out the workers. The family is negotiating with their own money, and so are the workers. They both have an incentive to reach a reasonable compromise.

Now, compare that situation to one in which government workers unionize and make demands. The workers and their union are represented by negotiators who have a definite interest in winning their demands; but the employers in this case do not have proper representation. The employers, the people who actually pay the workers salaries and benefits, are the taxpayers—us. Our representative in the negotiations is a politician or a group of politicians negotiating not with their own money, but with ours.

The union negotiators have a decided advantage in these negotiations in that unions can promise to deliver huge sums of money as campaign contributions plus a huge labor force to "volunteer" in a politician's campaigns. This offers no benefit to us taxpayers, the ones who will pay the salaries and other compensation, but offers great value personally to the people who are supposedly representing our interests. Thus, the union can easily co-opt our representatives and make them, in fact, their representatives in the negotiations. In other words, both sides are negotiating for the union's demands, and against our interests, now.

Recent evidence of how much power government worker unions have and are willing to wield against any officeholder who dares oppose their agenda is abundant in the Wisconsin Governor Scott Walker Recall attempt. While the unions did not succeed in that case, they certainly may have struck fear in the hearts of many other politicians who may not possess the courage and commitment that Governor Walker demonstrated. Nobody wants to walk into that buzz saw if they can avoid it.

> Libertarian John Stossel reported that the City of Detroit, which is bankrupt, employs a horseshoer. Of course, the city does not own any horses. When it was suggested that they did not need to be paying the $56,245 annual salary (including benefits), the union responded that the city needs more, not fewer, workers.

It is certainly obvious how far the defenders of the Bureaucracy are willing to go to oppose any diminishing of their power. Facts that came out during the battle in Wisconsin showed that the government workers were definitely not underpaid. In fact, they earn about double what they would be paid for the same work in the private sector. Many of the strikers and protesters were union teachers from the Wisconsin public schools systems. While the average income of a Wisconsin private-sector worker is about $30-40 thousand, The lowest-paid teacher protesting earned $68 thousand and the highest-paid teacher earned well over $100 thousand—and they were rioting and destroying public property to protest modest reforms that were necessary to avoid bankruptcy of Wisconsin.

SAMPLE DATA FOR SOME WISCONSIN SCHOOL DISTRICTS
Teacher Compensation - 2011

School District	Low Salary	High Salary	Avg. Salary	Fringe Ben.	Total Avg. Comp.
Abbotsford	34,986	70,821	47,923	15,291	63,214
Appleton	36,766.	72,742	58,716	28,504	87,220
Colfax	33,746	71,230	50,792	29,156	79,948
Fox Point	35,605	79,270	61,912	27,887	89,799
Nicolet	23,287	90,312	72,499	30,816	103,315

source: Wisconsin Department of Public Instruction

The above figures are for teachers only. Administrator salaries range up to over $120,000 with fringe benefit packages that range to over $40,000. The average salary of a retail store manager in Wisconsin at this same time was under $38,000 with a benefit package that is likely far inferior to those shown above for teachers.

Note: the overly-generous salaries and benefits of public school teachers are certainly not based on merit; in fact, the Department of Education has altered the philosophy of teaching such that a teacher need not know the subject matter he/she is teaching. It is not uncommon for a teacher in, say, math, to present canned lessons from a provided syllabus, issue prearranged assignments and tests, and grade the tests according to an answer sheet without ever actually understanding the material. Students may be forbidden or discouraged from asking questions of the teacher, who would not know the answers anyhow. The hallmark of a Bureaucracy is increased cost for decreased results.

Members of a Privileged Class always come to feel entitled to their status and ruthless in their defense of it.

The very powerful Bureaucracy (at all levels of government) now employs over fifteen percent (15%) of the voters in our country and they can be relied upon to almost always support protecting and increasing the power and privilege of the arising ruling class of which they are a part. Since each government employee's immediate family also benefits, we can pretty safely assume that about 30% of our voters have direct incentives to protect their personal interests and to support continuing expansion.

I have personally known public school teachers who sent their own children to private school. They worked for the high pay so as to be able to afford to keep their kids *out of* the public school system. I have also known private school teachers who left high-paying jobs as teachers in the public school system to take a 50% pay cut to teach in private schools because of their personal integrity.

BIGGER THAN THE LEFT OR THE RIGHT

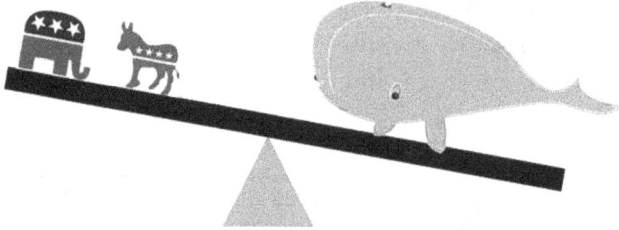

The Bureaucracy can overpower even our duly elected government officials, regardless which party they are from.

We struggle and fight to elect good candidates who believe as we do that the Constitution must be preserved; but more-and-more I am feeling that we are electing mere figureheads. Elections are becoming almost a symbolic gesture with real power being held by people we can not vote for or against who hold us and our elected officials in contempt.

William J. Murray is Chairman of the Religious Freedom Coalition and President of GING-PAC, a Washington-based political action committee. He observes:

> *"My decades inside the Washington Beltway have taught me one certain truth: Once government creates a massive program, it never goes away regardless of the party in power. Lyndon Johnson's war on poverty is still with us, and a greater percentage of people are below the poverty line now than when the program began billions of tax dollars ago. Ronald Reagan's 'Star Wars' program to create the perfect missile defense system against an attack by the Soviet Union has outlasted the Soviet Union by more than a decade. George W. Bush was going to eliminate large bureaucratic programs; instead, he created No Child Left Behind, plus a new entitlement for prescription drugs that will be with us until the last copy of the Constitution is burned.*
>
> *Ethanol, which has been declared even by the environmentalists as a mistake because it causes more pollution than gasoline, is required by law to be used by cars,*

trucks and boats in spite of the fact that even Al Gore has turned against subsidizing ethanol.

"These giant programs never go away after they are created because of the number of people whose careers become dependent on them. Take ethanol for example. The Renewable Fuels Association states that there are 90,000 people directly employed in the production of ethanol, and additionally it 'supports' 401,000 jobs."

Your author with Bill Murray at a fundraiser event we arranged for a conservative candidate a decade ago

Short of an actual reform of the Administrative Law that provides extra-constitutional authority to federal agencies, the Bureaucracy has the might to overpower any attempts by even the highest elected officials to rein it in. Regarding the Affordable Healthcare Act, Murray adds:

"This is why ObamaCare is never going away regardless of who is in power. The legislation created hundreds of new federal commissions and boards. The insurance industry and corporations hired tens of thousands of support personnel to manage the requirements of ObamaCare. New entitlements such as an expanded CHIP (Medicaid for kids whose parents are at three times the poverty level or less) can't be taken away once they are in place. There are already hundreds of thousands of government jobs not only at the federal level, but at the state and local levels as well, plus those in private industry, that are at stake.

"What about the Republican plans to 'repeal' ObamaCare? Read the fine print: The Republican plan is to 'repeal and

replace'. *If there is no replacement, the jobs vanish. What will Republicans really do with ObamaCare the next time they come into power? Easy Answer: They will shave a little in some places and add a little in other places, change the name of it and declare it fixed.*

When does it all end?

"When there are so many people standing in line for handouts that there are not enough people left to man the give-away windows." – William J. Murray

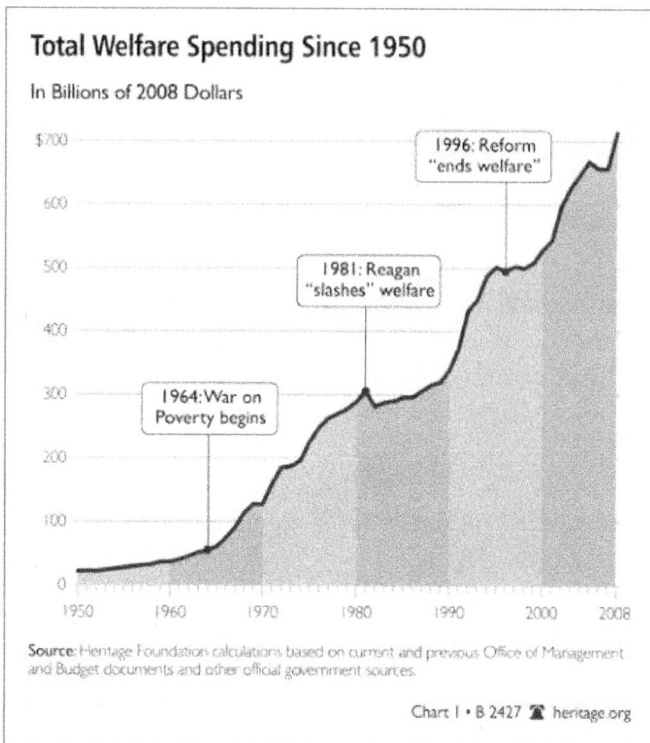

Total Welfare Spending Since 1950

In Billions of 2008 Dollars

- 1996: Reform "ends welfare"
- 1981: Reagan "slashes" welfare
- 1964: War on Poverty begins

Source: Heritage Foundation calculations based on current and previous Office of Management and Budget documents and other official government sources.

Chart I • B 2427 ☎ heritage.org

This Welfare Spending chart from Heritage Foundation illustrates Murray's point.

According to a recent Wall Street Journal report the price of corn is up almost 80% largely as a result of the forced use of corn to produce ethanol to add to gasoline. Thus, the price of food is increased, the performance (fuel economy) of combustion engines is decreased, and the price of automobiles is increased to accommodate this inferior fuel mandated by a Bureaucracy more interested in demonstrating its arbitrary power than in improving our lives. As of the time I am writing this, our government has refused to allow the rule requiring ethanol in our gasoline to abate in spite of reports that the recent drought will result in a shortage of corn and that starvation may occur in some other countries that rely on buying corn from the US for food.

THE COCKROACHES

Congressman Steve Stockman was elected to office in 1994 from Texas Congressional District 9. He was a part of the huge Republican/Conservative sweep. He was ranked one of the two most conservative members of the House by the opposing party. Because of a massive redistricting in Texas, District 9 was altered radically and he was not able to win re-election in the new District 9. At the time of this writing, he is the Representative for Texas District 36 (which includes much of the same territory as District 9 did long ago) and is the first Representative for this newly created district that resulted from the recent redistricting of Texas to accommodate four more seats to represent the increased population shown for Texas in the last Census.

During his first term in office, Stockman proposed reforms that featured sunset clauses in all new regulations, much as I am proposing as a part of the reform promoted in this book. Stockman is keenly aware of the

Your author with Congressman Stockman during a mid-90's campaign. My older daughter is wearing a campaign T-shirt.

dangers of the bloated Bureaucracy, the Fourth Branch of our government. The Bureaucrats are also well aware of it—so much so that they have established a society they call The Cockroaches.

The name of the society stems from the fact that politicians may come and go and wars may start and end; but the Bureaucracy will always be there. No matter whether Republicans or

Democrats, Conservatives or Liberals, are in control of elected offices, the bureaucrats, like the insect they chose to name themselves after, will survive and continue making rules and regulations. Presumably the science fiction image of a world in which mankind and most animal life has been destroyed by nuclear war, but in which cockroaches survive unchanged from how they have been since the age of the dinosaurs inspired the name. Needless to say, The Cockroaches do not publicly advertise the existence of their semi-secret society.

Stockman also points out that Bureaucrats have a strong incentive for passing more and more rules and regulations, regardless whether or not they are in America's best interests. Passing many new regulations demonstrates that they are *doing something* and are needed. It justifies the bureaucrats' existence.

> *"Today, most 'laws' actually are rules and regulations enacted by bureaucrats in government agencies, not statutes passed by elected lawmakers. Even when Congress does pass legislation, such as the Dodd-Frank financial reform law or Obamacare, lawmakers leave many blanks and expect rule-makers to fill them in. That means the bureaucracy, peopled with federal 'experts,' essentially exists as an unelected fourth branch of government."*—Heritage Foundation President Ed Feulner

We can be sure that Stockman, along with other great friends of our cause in office at both the national and state levels, will remain allies of our mission as we fight for reform. In fact, I am asking each for his or her personal assurance.

11. Seduction of Power

"...if you want to test a man's character, give him power." –
Abraham Lincoln

Power is seductive and addictive. Men who attain it tend to always want more. With the exception of a few very unusual persons, they will use what power they have to gain ever more. This is true at every level of government and it is true regardless which political party or philosophy is in control at any given time. There is no doubt that American liberals move much more aggressively to increase the power of government when they are in control; but even when Conservatives are in control the expansion of government continues, albeit slightly more slowly. The Bureaucracy has become so powerful as to be able to resist even the best efforts of the most conservative, limited-government-minded, and Constitution-inspired elected officials. It continues to expand itself in *any* political environment using any means it can.

The number of government employees had grown to over 21.2 million by the beginning of 2010 and has continued to grow since.

The graph I have posted here is from the US Census Bureau. It shows that even during the presidency of Ronald Reagan, the bureaucracy continued to expand. Then, under the presidency of the less-conservative Bush, it expanded faster. Under Clinton and the younger Bush the rapid rate of growth continued. If you agree that the expansion of the Fourth Branch is destroying our nation, you must also agree that just electing conservative politicians *merely slows down*, but does not halt, our march toward destruction. What we need is not merely to halt it; but to reverse it. We must do more than just elect Conservatives!

State and Local Employment Totals
Separated by Education and Noneducation
for Census Years 1957–2007

Millions

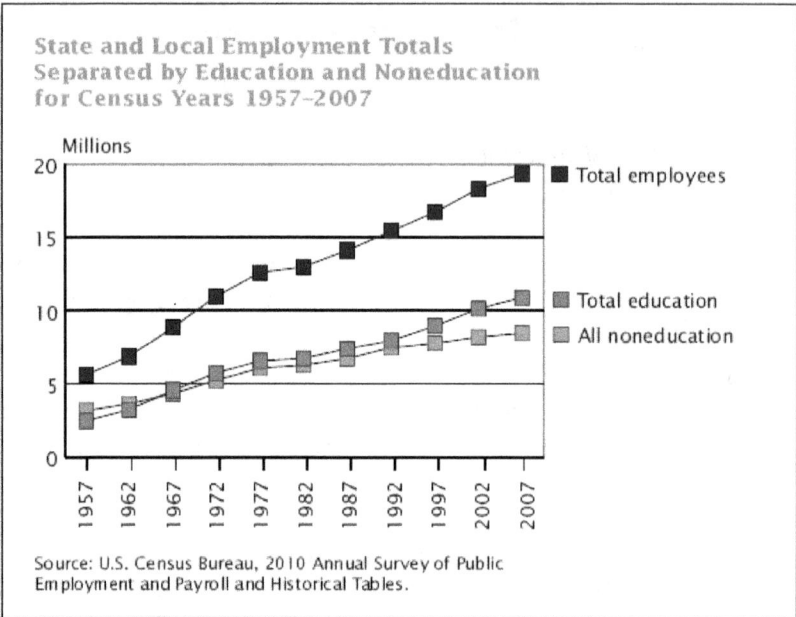

Source: U.S. Census Bureau, 2010 Annual Survey of Public
Employment and Payroll and Historical Tables.

We tend to think of our federal government as a collection of politicians, including 435 Members of the House of Representatives, 100 Senators, 1 President, and 1 Vice President. We might even include from 2,000 to 4,000 (depending on your definition) federal judges, justices, and magistrates. What is missing from that list is approximately 2-3 million federal employees (if you add state and local government employees the number is over 20 million). Some of those federal workers do some sort of technical job; but many are administrators, managers, and supervisors. All have a vested interest in the continued expansion of government.

Even if we were to elect all small-government Conservatives to office, we will have installed a few hundred people to struggle against millions who continually push to expand the size and power of the bureaucracy that employs them. We might note that recent data shows that government employees are paid much higher salaries than their private-sector counterparts and have much more generous benefits plus job security that is unmatched anywhere else in our society. This attests to the massive influence they have over our government and our entire nation. It also gives them a strong incentive to resist any reduction in the power wielded by the bloated bureaucracy.

In the past decade, while the number of private-sector jobs has grown only 1%, the number of federal government jobs has increased by 15%. Even more significant is that the average total compensation, including benefits, for private-sector workers nationwide is about $60,000. The average total compensation for government workers is over $120,000 — more than double!

> Note: the economic strength of a nation can be expressed by its Gross National Product (GNP), the sum of all it produces each year. Government does not produce anything; it is to a nation what overhead is to a business enterprise. Thus, as the size of our government increases, the economic strength of our nation declines.

The chart produced by TruthfulPolitics.com shows graphically how, since the New Deal era, even during conservative administrations government growth continues. This is evidence enough that the systemic cancer will spread with or without the help of liberal elected officials and in spite of attempts to contain it by Conservatives. Average growth during Democrat administrations is just over three percent (3%), during Republican control, just over two percent (2%) with the WWII years excluded. The Bureaucracy truly has broken loose from any tethers it may have ever had placed upon it by the Legislature or even by Presidents. Electing Conservatives is not enough.

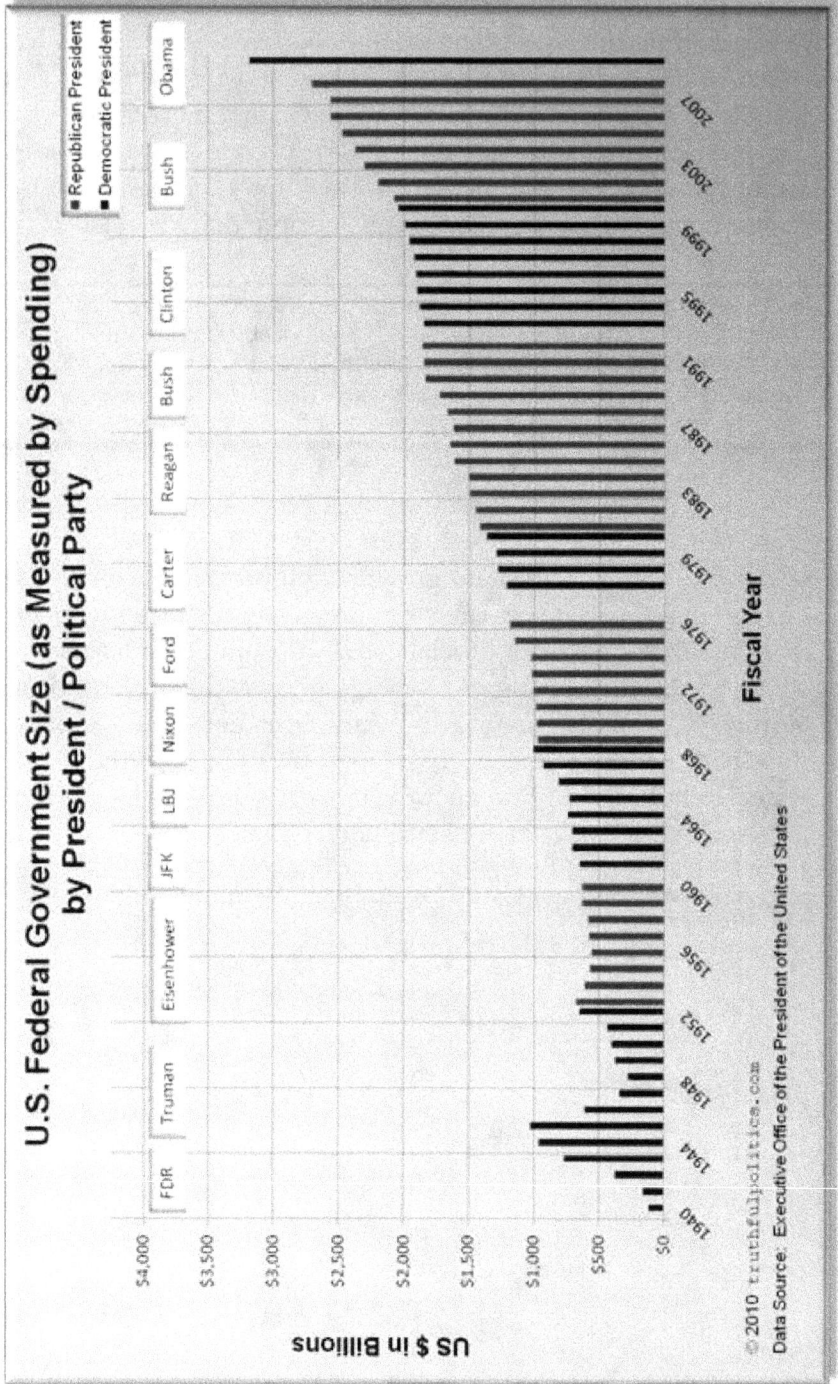

U.S. Federal Government Size (as Measured by Spending) by President / Political Party

© 2010 truthfulpolitics.com

Data Source: Executive Office of the President of the United States

Lee

THE REAL POWER IN GOVERNMENT

Perhaps the best and most recognizable example to illustrate how powerful bureaucrats can be and how they can deflect controls by even the highest elected officials would be J. Edgar Hoover.

Hoover, as a founder of the FBI and its first director, held on to his powerful post nearly 50 years until he died in 1972. Even Presidents dared not cross him. He reputedly gathered and stored information about high political figures and routinely ignored laws restricting how information may be legally obtained. No Senator, Representative, or President wanted to be on Hoover's bad side. Certainly none would ever have the courage to suggest replacing him with another appointee—hence the de-facto permanent appointment.

Hoover was one of the most powerful bureaucrats in the world

Though he was not elected to any office and was nominally reporting to the President, he was able to manipulate our entire government from the shadows. Because there was no term limit on his position (at the time), he had the equivalent of a lifetime reign over Democrats, Republicans, and anyone else he cared to control. Interestingly, like another major political figure today, he did not have a birth certificate on record.

Hoover was admittedly a special case among bureaucrats and the ability to blackmail political figures might be limited to a few positions such as his; but all bureaucrats have tools to employ to exert influence over elected politicians. They can make policy decisions or massage statistics that they report to reflect positively or negatively on a public official or to support some government program. For example, not including as income Welfare, Food Stamps, Medicaid, and other government payments to people greatly inflates the number of Americans classified as being below the poverty line, justifying more money allocated to "fight poverty." They can influence the political support of thousands of their subordinates and of businesses that they can affect through regulation. Unions of government workers can spend millions of dollars to help or to oppose a politician. Agencies can "leak" sensitive information that would help or hinder a politician's re-election campaign. Only the most courageous elected officials will risk making enemies in the Bureaucracy.

At the time I am writing this, teachers in Chicago just returned from a strike at the beginning of the school year, leaving thousands of students and their parents adrift. Their complaint was that the 16% pay raise package offered by the City of Chicago over the next four years was insufficient and they do not want to be held accountable for student test scores on standardized tests. This is in spite of the facts that Chicago students are among the worst educated in the nation, Chicago is on the verge of bankruptcy, the median income of Chicago residents is about $44,000, and the median income of Chicago teachers is about $76,000. It is just weeks before the national elections and the President of the United States was forced to take the side of the teachers because he needs their support in the election. He dares not offend so powerful a force as the education bureaucracy, regardless how outlandish their demands.

TARGETING THE INNOCENT

There was a time when a government agency had to at least *allege* that you had done something wrong in order to penalize you. Those days are gone. Since the "War on Drugs" was initiated, the Department of Justice has had the authority to seize private property of persons *suspected* of being guilty (remember when "innocent until proven guilty" was still the rule?) of drug trafficking.

The Fourth Amendment to our Constitution guarantees us protection from warrantless searches and seizures of our property; but DOJ and DEA are no longer bound by that provision of the Constitution.

Would you object to the government seizing property that a convicted drug trafficker used in his trade? Probably not. Neither would I. But, being convicted and just being accused or suspected are not the same thing. Now, to make it even worse, the property of innocent bystanders is taken by government agents. The Wall Street Journal reported about a New York businessman, James Lieto, whose cash ($392,000) was taken because he had hired an armored car company to transport it and the armored car company was *suspected* of distributing drugs. Lieto was not, and never had been, suspected of doing anything wrong; but the government agency refused to return his money. New DOJ rules now also allow them to seize all firearms from a home in which any occupant is suspected of having even small amounts of a drug—regardless who owns those firearms. That nullifies both the Fourth and the Second Amendments in one stroke.

Remember, these rules are used to seize property from people who are *not even suspected* of wrongdoing.

12. Invitation to Corruption

The ability to create agencies and to appoint heads of those agencies, mostly done by the Executive Branch, is an open invitation to corruption and cronyism. Although legislators have tried to halt the practice of politically-motivated appointments by the Executive, their attempts do not seem to have had much effect. We need only review the long list of unqualified men and women with dubious histories who have been appointed to high positions or have been given posts as "czars" in the current Administration to see just how ineffective those attempts were.

Appointments to reward cronies or to pay back supporters of ones political campaign or agenda are called "Patronage Appointments" and are common. Many supporters of a political candidate's campaign give their support with the expectation of receiving a powerful position in return after the candidate wins. This leads to yet another corruption of the system.

Having "friendly" heads of powerful agencies and programs oftentimes leads to an abuse of the agency or program for political ends. Since the appointee has received a valuable, powerful position from the President (or other politician), he is somewhat obligated to "play ball" in return. This was evident from the very start with the New Deal creations.

FDR had created the WPA (Works Progress Administration), which gave government jobs to many unemployed Americans. Then, in the elections of 1938, the agency led WPA workers to aid candidates from FDR's party, much the way union workers are often used in elections today. This led to a law called the "Hatch Act," which forbade government workers from participating in partisan politics. Of course, it is the Department of Justice (DOJ) that must enforce this law and <u>DOJ is itself headed by a political appointee</u> and the department has been guilty of highly politicized hiring practices to ensure that it is staffed by people sympathetic to the current administration. A current demonstration of the ability of DOJ to act politically, rather than constitutionally, is its failure to enforce the Defense of Marriage Act (DOMA) and numerous Immigration Laws in order to aid the current President with some of his core constituency, gay marriage advocates and those promoting amnesty for illegal aliens. Recently, DOJ even issued a hiring directive giving an extreme advantage to persons with mental deficiencies or emotional problems. Such persons are easy to manipulate to hew uncritically to the liberal agenda. The Hatch Act seems to work very effectively against conservative or Republican candidates and not so well against Democrat candidates.

Another example of the corrupting effect of this power to create agencies and to appoint heads is the NLRB (National Labor Relations Board). FDR created it to support unionism and his party continues to support the NLRB and unions.

Recently, the NLRB sued The Boeing Company for its plan to build parts for its 787 Dreamliner aircraft in a plant in South Carolina instead of another plant in Washington. The reason was because the Washington plant is unionized and the South Carolina plant is non-union. The federal agency is obviously lending itself to forced unionization of American companies in spite of the fact that the SC workers, who had once been union, voted by a large majority to leave the International Association of Machinists (IAM).

In return, unions support them with everything from huge cash contributions to free campaign labor to "enforcement" activities that include intimidation of voters and campaign workers and volunteers. In the recent failed attempt to recall Republican Governor Scott Walker in Wisconsin, labor unions (from many states) spent an unprecedented amount, estimated to be about $20 million, of their members' money attacking one governor and a handful of state legislators.

Agencies with regulating powers over an industry also have very effective ways to coerce both principles and workers in that industry to support a certain political candidate or position, or to offer special favors or outright bribes. A regulating agency can punish an entire industry with unreasonable, impossible-to-comply-with rules that could literally shut the industry down.

The current rules regarding methane and carbon dioxide emissions are being used to cripple the natural gas drilling industry and coal-fired electric generation industry. Perhaps if these industries had made sufficiently large political contributions to the right political party, they would not now have to contend with these problems.

> *The current economic malaise was started by what is known as the "Sub-prime Lending Crisis." One of the chief offenders causing the crisis was a company called Countrywide Financial Corp., which sold a huge number of loans to Fannie Mae. In order to enhance its influence among legislators and regulators, Countrywide made hundreds of very attractive special loan deals with them and even had a formal program called the "VIP Loan Program" to buy influence all the way up to the US Senate (Chris Dodd) and Fannie Mae executives.*

Big business is not ignorant of the immense power that federal agencies possess. Even though many of these agencies were established with the stated purpose of reining in abuses by big business, many huge corporations spend millions of dollars currying favor with government and lobbying for regulations that stifle their competition, especially from smaller upstarts.

In a 2011 survey of small businesses among its members, the National Federation of Independent Business reported that respondents cited "regulations and red tape" being second only to "poor sales" as the biggest problem they faced. Nineteen percent of businesses reported that regulations were their number one problem. Smaller businesses are less well equipped to deal with the burdens the government places on them.

A lot of people have an image of big government as an opponent of big business. This inaccurate picture is fostered largely by Liberals who promote the idea that government must be powerful in order to restrain corporate misbehavior. Conservatives also fall for this line of thinking quite often. But, big government regularly works hand-in-hand in alliance with giant corporations. These giant corporations may represent themselves to be "American Business"; but frequently are actually trans-national companies that may have started in our country long ago, but now operate worldwide—often employing many times more people in other countries than in the USA.

> *A recent egregious example of how the Big Business-Big Government nexus functions to benefit them, not us, is the appointment of Jeffrey Immelt, CEO of General Electric, as Barack Obama's top economic advisor on creation of American jobs. Immelt is responsible for moving thousands of American jobs, and entire divisions of GE, to China. He has done this while GE receives billions of dollars in tax breaks for allegedly creating American jobs producing "green" technology. Of course, that technology is manufactured in China, not in America. Not only is that a transfer of jobs out of the US, it is a transfer of technology that was developed in the US. Some of that technology is of military importance to boot. The title "Jobs Czar" has as much meaning as the name of the "Ministry of Truth" in George Orwell's book, "1984."*

Possibly the most outrageous example of the corruption that abounds in our Bureaucracy can be seen in the "Stimulus" spending of billions of our tax dollars. Much of the money was given to foreign companies that actually compete with American companies. This was done in the name of creating American jobs; but actually has cost us American jobs and created jobs for Mexican, Chinese, Thai, Vietnamese, or other non-US workers around the world. Even infrastructure projects inside the US are being given to foreign, often Chinese, companies and paid for by our tax dollars.

> The "stimulus" tactic employed by our government and The Federal Reserve known as Quantitative Easing (QE) is actually just "printing" money (by computer, not printing press) and giving it to a few favored giant companies. It actually enriches those few companies while devaluing everyone else's money.

The Chevrolet Volt is sold for about $41,000 and costs over $200,000 in subsidies to build. The subsidies are, of course, given from our tax dollars. Though it is touted as an American-made vehicle, it is actually only assembled in the US from components mostly made elsewhere. Most notable is the lithium battery made in South Korea. That is the battery that is said to cost more than the car costs to replace when it runs out and that might spontaneously erupt into flames if damaged.

General Motors received $50 billion of taxpayer money and its bondholders were essentially wiped out in the government bailout of GM. In 2011 GM's CEO, Dan Akerson, boasted in a speech given in Communist China that now seventy percent (70%) of the vehicles GM builds are built in China. GM now has eleven (11) Chinese manufacturing facilities in joint ventures with the Communist government. Further, the US Government is GM's largest customer for vehicles. American taxpayers, stockholders, and bondholders have all been soaked for billions of dollars, and continue to be soaked, because of a cozy crony capitalistic relationship between big business and big government.

It is often true that government, the Bureaucracy in particular, acts in ways very harmful to small- and medium-sized businesses and to common citizens and taxpayers; but in ways very beneficial to huge (usually international) corporations that can afford to buy influence. That is partially because the concept of *management by experts*, which we will discuss next, leads government to appoint people taken from high-level management in giant companies to be heads of federal agencies and departments, or to be trusted advisors. (I have already noted that these giant companies and the managers taken from them do not necessarily have American interests foremost in their hearts.) Most of us are aware, for instance, that a very disproportionate number of President Obama's appointees in financial and economic positions all come from one source: Goldman Sachs. Of course, that was also true in the administration of George W. Bush. Both these presidents had a hand in the massive bailout program that benefited not us citizens, not small businesses, but a few huge financial institutions — like Goldman Sachs!

Until the house of cards collapsed, Countrywide Financial Corp. was actually serving as an advisor to the House Financial Services Committee and Senate Banking Committee, helping to craft the regulation of its own industry. You can be certain that they placed their corporate wellbeing at the top of their priorities and utilized their influence with powerful government watchdogs in order to further their interests rather than those of the country.

When government agencies impose regulations that are very difficult for businesses to comply with, it is often the case that the giant companies are much more able to meet those requirements while smaller businesses simply can not. This puts many small competitors out of business, with the benefits accruing to the big companies that helped craft these regulations in the first place. Thus, government regulation becomes a force for *encouraging* monopoly in spite of the fact that one of the chief arguments supporting government regulation of business decades ago was to *prevent* monopolies and trusts from forming.

> One example of how government programs work in favor of giant companies and against smaller competitors is the Farm Bill and agricultural subsidies. Most of the benefit goes to huge agricultural corporations, not to small farmers. This has contributed to a decline in the number of family farms over the past decades. Their farm land has been merged into the large corporate farm operations that receive billions of taxpayer dollars and are insulated from the possibility of failure while small farms are failing all around them. In 1940 about 30 million Americans lived on about 6 million farms, today about 6 million Americans live on about 2 million farms.

The 2010 Dodd–Frank Wall Street Reform and Consumer Protection Act is a recent example. A massive restructuring of all regulation and oversight of financial institutions, it expands the definition of the types of companies to be regulated, adds daunting amounts of new reporting, and requires lenders to "encourage" borrowing by "disadvantaged" groups of persons. This last feature has similarities to the Community Reinvestment Act that was the underlying cause of the sub-prime lending collapse that triggered the massive recession we are still struggling through.

No lender naturally wants to make loans to people who are unlikely to repay them; but coercion by government forces them to do so. If the bad loans that result collapse and push the lender into a loss position, the giant companies with close ties to government agencies and their heads know that some sort of government rescue will save them while the smaller institutions will be allowed to fail. There is no reason to believe that any consumer protection will result from this Act, in spite of its name. There is good reason to conclude that it creates a partnership between the mega financial institutions and the federal government.

> *I should repeat here that the definition of Socialism and Communism is government ownership of the means of production. The definition of Fascism is nominal private ownership with actual government control. There is really not much difference in the effects. They are simply two variants of Statism. We should easily recognize the fact that excessive government regulation constitutes government control; hence: Fascism.*

HOW TO ROB A BANK

There is a book entitled "The Best Way to Rob a Bank is to Own One." It is one of several books chronicling the role that poor and corrupted regulation contributed massively to the Bank and S&L collapses in the mid 1980's. Without delving into all the details, I will focus on the fact that there were many banks in Texas that were declared insolvent and shut down, with their assets being liquidated at a fraction of their worth.

Many persons "in the know" believe that the crisis was at least partially engineered by collusion between regulators and some giant East Coast banks that were envious of the success of some banks in Texas and wanted to get control of that market like they had control of the rest of the US.

The crisis erupted in full at the exact middle of the decade, January, 1986. It was set up by ridiculously lax regulations prior to that time. Bank charters were given out willy-nilly with very little requirement that the bank operators even knew how to run a bank. That resulted in a number of very questionable banks being established among the numbers of very strong banks.

Banks are required to maintain a Loan Loss Reserve that is set based on that bank's recent history and portfolio of bad loans. Bank regulators have the power to declare any loan to be a bad loan with virtually no explanation required. Each loan classified as being bad increases the requirement for a Loan Loss Reserve, of course. A bank has to tap its own Capital Account to supplement the Loan Loss Reserve account in order to remain "solvent."

Bank regulators at the time arbitrarily decided that many good loans in targeted banks were, in their judgement, bad loans, thus forcing the banks to tap out their own Capital Accounts.

Once the bank is out of capital and can no longer reach into that account to add to the Loan Loss Account, the bank is declared "insolvent." Thus, hundreds of banks were forced into insolvency and had their assets taken over by special government-created corporations, such as the Resolution Trust Corporation, and liquidated at fire-sale prices.

Then you could watch the signs in front of hundreds of small banks being replaced with signs for some giant Eastern banking corporation.

Interestingly, while there were banks all over the US in more-or-less the identical situation, special treatment was carved out for banks in Texas, it was called the "Southwest Plan." It provided for particularly harsh dealings with Texas banks while banks in other states were given time to work out of their circumstance and many did.

Many old Texas bankers who were in the business back then say they have no doubt that there was collaboration between the big Eastern banking corporations and the government regulators.

If you thought that just electing conservative politicians to office would cure the problem (as one candidate for office once told me), this is an example of how the regulators do their harm regardless whether Conservatives or Liberals are in control. This happened during the administration of Ronald Reagan! The out-of-control Bureaucracy is a menace that overshadows even Left-Right politics.

ORGANIZED CRIME

Another manifestation of corruption fostered by the unholy alliance of government and business is the attraction to organized crime. With government bureaucrats having the power to control and direct billions of dollars of other people's money, there is a tremendous opportunity for organized crime syndicates to tap into the fountain of riches and to subvert the government agents whose job it is to prevent just such misdirection of our tax dollars so that they can continue to operate with impunity. It is estimated by many that thirty-percent or more (30%+) of Medicaid and Medicare payments go to huge criminal organizations that are often not challenged because they have corrupted and intimidated the government watchdogs using bribery, threats, and violence. So powerful are they, that some of the leaders of the organized crime rings involved are connected to foreign governments and international organized crime operations. One recent example of such an organization that was shut down by the FBI is the Mirzoyan–Terdjanian Organization , a violent Mafia-like group that had criminal and political connections in Armenia. It was fraudulently milking the Medicare and Medicaid systems for many millions of dollars a year.

Other criminal organizations involved in Medicare and Medicaid fraud are connected to Russian, Nigerian, and other foreign Mafia-like groups. The pickings are just too easy for them to resist.

Again, prevention of monopolies was one of the best examples of the need for some regulation by government (see Need for Regulations below). Ironically, the excessive regulation we are experiencing tends to create monopolies. It is nearly impossible to compete in a marketplace with a business that is partnered with government because government can impose more and more obstacles in front of any competitor and it can subsidize the business with unlimited tax dollars that its competition does not have access to (think of Fannie Mae and Freddie Mac for example). Government itself is a monopoly. Thus it is best to minimize the connections between it and any private sector enterprises.

The authority to tax or to regulate is the authority to control or to destroy. This is a fact that will not go unnoticed by ambitious politicians and bureaucrats. Power indeed does corrupt and the current Administrative Law that lets a President (or the Legislature) create agencies and then empower those agencies to act virtually unchecked and unrestrained by Constitutional limits puts altogether too much power into the hands of the central government and the Bureaucracy it spawns.

13. Government by Experts

One of the underlying principles that underpins the bureaucracy is the assumption that various aspects of governing are done best by experts. This thinking goes all the way back in history to tribal governments that were led by "wise elders." It is easy to make the case that the person who makes decisions about, say, water quality should be an expert in the subject. In fact, though, this is a very dangerous assumption. In The Road to Serfdom, Friedrich A. Hayek explains that government by experts is a direct route to statist tyranny, calling it "the fatal conceit."

The belief that the expert knows best leads to the argument that he or she must have more and more authority in order to implement the solution to the problem. Ultimately, that means unrestricted, unquestioned power. The expert becomes a minor tyrant resenting any challenge to his wisdom and authority. Views opposing his or hers are soon deemed to be unpatriotic or seditious and, eventually, unlawful.

The "expert" individual gradually comes to supplant the office and thus he becomes irreplaceable. Policies are no longer "the department's policy"; but "Mr. Expert's policy." The concept of Rule of Law gives way to a Rule of Man, with all the shortcomings and perils that go with it. As a recent example, if you have dealt with mortgage lenders in the past few years you may have heard of the "Obama Loan Modificaton Plan" or other such programs that are identified with the man, not the bank or even the government agency that administers the plan. While most of us will likely agree that Mr. Obama is not likely a genuine expert on mortgage loans, he is being held up as if he were and being presented as the benefactor who will modify your loan. The implication is that if he were not there to save you, you would be stuck.

We can assume with fairly high certainty that even the tribal wise men took advantage of their positions for personal gain and to increase their powers and tried to present themselves as being personally indispensable to the survival of the people.

Experts certainly do have their place. They are very useful as staffers and advisers. In fact, much better decisions usually result from considering with an open mind varying opinions from several experts. If the head of a program or agency is legitimately an expert, he or she is likely to be much less open-minded or willing to consider opposing ideas. Also, most head-of-department positions are actually more general in nature than what an expert in one specific discipline might be trained to deal with. The higher the position, the more general it becomes. The best police commissioner is not necessarily the person who scores highest on the firing range.

There is an expression: "To a hammer, every problem looks like a nail.." A person who is an expert in one field will naturally approach every problem as if it was in his field. A more effective problem solver would take a much broader view of the issue and then solicit input and ideas from a variety of experts in many different fields, then weigh the pros and cons of all approaches.

In business we sometimes see brilliant experts who become the leaders of successful companies. But those experts usually abandon their roles as experts in a very narrow field and train themselves in much broader management and marketing skills. They also try to hire other experts in specific areas who are even better than they themselves were. In other words, they overcome the impediment of being an expert in order to become effective at a higher level.

The idea that these regulatory federal agencies should be headed by people with particular expertise in the industries they regulate leads to the appointments of high, powerful positions to people drawn from the largest companies in those industries. That creates a nexus between big government and big business which works to the disadvantage of the most important businesses in America, small- and medium-sized businesses.

While it may seem like an extreme example, I must refer to one well-known transfer of identity from an organization to a personality that contributed to massive disaster. The *Greater German Youth Movement* in Germany morphed into the *Hitler Youth* because of the immense popularity (within certain groups) of the man who projected himself as the saviour of their nation. When such transitions occur, whether it involves a formal name change or not, the influence of an individual begins to eclipse the mission of the organization. An example right here in the USA that most of you can remember was J. Edgar Hoover and the FBI. Mr. Hoover did not need to change the name of the FBI to his name in order to aggrandize his personal power to blatantly ignore laws and to use the resources of our government to pursue his own personal agenda.

Governance by experts is not a desirable thing.

14. Need for Regulations

"Liberty, too, must be limited in order to be possessed" –
Edmund Burke

You might surmise from much I have already written that I am opposed to regulations *per se*. That is not so! I recognize the necessity for some regulations. There are some problems that only the government is powerful enough to deal with. For some, I would even go so far as to say that only the central (federal) government can effectively handle the problem. For example: preventing trusts and monopolies in commerce and industry.

I am also not opposed to the existence of a bureaucracy. The law and elected officials can not attend to the many, many issues and sub issues that are necessarily a part of a complex society. There is a legitimate need for lower-level agencies to deal with those details. There are also instances in which the bureaucracy needs authority to regulate something that would not fall within the Enumerated Powers defined in the Constitution.

The Federal Trade Commission combats monopolies and trusts

For example, our economic system, the best in the world, is Capitalism. Capitalism offers any average person the opportunity to reach unlimited success and the rewards attendant to it. That also means that it is possible for one individual or organization, or several organizations working in concert, to achieve a monopoly on some necessary commodity and to thereby control prices and to block competition to the detriment of the entire country. Obviously, that is a huge potential problem.

Ironically, government, which is itself a monopoly, is the only entity with sufficient power to break up or prevent commercial monopolies and trusts (cooperative agreements among competitors to fix pricing or otherwise behave as if they were a single monopoly) in our economy.

Similarly, some industries have the capability to affect air or water quality because of pollutants that they might release. Since our water and air are natural, national resources, it is appropriate for government to establish standards to control damage done by those industries or similar activities. If the resource is local to a single state, then it seems appropriate for the State government to exercise its authority; but if the resource is shared by multiple states only the federal government could effectively act.

There are more examples of appropriate circumstances for government regulation. In fact, even in his ground-breaking book, The Road To Serfdom, Friedrich A. Hayek concedes such a need. However, that does not argue for unrestrained exercise of government power into more and more intrusive aspects of our lives. Neither does it argue for regulations designed not for the benefit of our citizens; but for the benefit of the government which seeks greater control over its subjects. Surely a balance can be struck that accommodates the interests of both the needs of society and of individual liberty.

DEVIL IN THE DETAILS

The Bureaucracy is a necessary part of government of any nation. The Legislature can make laws, usually, only at a general level. There needs to be a hierarchy of officials who break those laws down into details and actually execute what the Legislature has made a law.

For instance, if the Legislature passes a law to protect our forests by requiring lumber harvesting companies to replenish what they have harvested there needs to be an agency that will define what constitutes "replenishing." Does planting one seed for each tree cut down suffice? Does planting ten, or twenty? Should there be some provision to require that they replant properly so that the seeds have a better chance to sprout and grow? Should the requirements be different for harvesting hardwoods from harvesting pine? The Members of the House and Senate can not craft their laws to so fine a level of detail. Maybe the Forest Service agency should handle those details.

The problem, though, comes when the agency begins to reach too far beyond its proper function, or when its administrators act on behalf of certain companies at the expense of others because of political considerations (or bribery), or when they allow themselves to be used as a weapon to punish political enemies or to reward political friends.

> *"The Environmental Protection Agency on a near daily basis issues new regulations clearly out of their purview in order to modify and change environmental laws previously passed and to impose a radical green agenda never approved by Congress. The same is true of the Energy and Interior Departments among many others." – Steve McCann, writing for The American Thinker*

In a recent and ongoing incident, the Justice Department (DOJ) has been used to harass a particular manufacturer of guitars — the only major non-union manufacturer of guitars. Gibson competes with Fender and other makers of guitars; but is a non-union company. Guitar makers purchase exotic woods from other countries for certain parts of their instruments, Gibson is no exception.

NASA was established in response to Russia's Sputnik

Gibson's plant has been raided, shut down, fined, and nearly put out of business for supposedly violating the law of another country regarding the requirement that a certain amount of indigenous labor must be included into the value of any wood products exported. Mind you, this is not a US law; it is a foreign country's law that should apply to the sellers of the wood, not the buyers. None of the union shops making guitars have been similarly attacked by DOJ, although they all purchase exactly the same products. This is an obvious corruption of a major federal agency for purely political purposes.

But, probably the most obvious corruption of a federal agency for political objectives was the attempted redirection of the National Aeronautics and Space Administration (NASA) (formed in 1958 in response to Russia's Sputnik Earth-orbiting satellite) to focus on outreach to Muslims worldwide rather than to matters of space travel. It is difficult to imagine any rationalization for that on-the-fly re-tasking of a major agency; but power-drunk Statists no longer seem to feel the need to justify anything they do. They feel entitled to do as they please, asking permission from no one, explaining nothing, and apologizing never.

A law that sounds perfectly proper and reasonable can be administered in grotesque ways because of the ability of the Bureaucracy to define the details of what that law means. As an example, I do not think that many of us would object to the law making it illegal to threaten the President's life or to violently overthrow our government. That sounds reasonable and prudent to most of us. However, when the administrators refine the definition of "to threaten the President" to include any speech opposing or even disagreeing with any policy of the President's, most of us will agree that they have gone too far and that this was never what was intended by the law.

Sometimes the nonsensical regulations that spew forth from our out-of-control Bureaucracy might be humorous, if they were not so damaging to our nation. Recently the EPA ruled that a substance called "cellulosic ethanol" must be added to our petroleum fuels. The problem is that cellulosic ethanol does not exist, it is a hypothetical substance that has not yet been invented or discovered. So much for the theoretical benefits of governance by "experts."

Almost any law must be written in general enough terms that it will be vulnerable to a liberal interpretation and distortion by those who have the power to decide what it means in specifics. Federal agencies then have the power to decide what that law means in detail. The Devil is certainly in the Details.

Pharmaceutical companies complain that it takes years and hundreds of millions of dollars to get approval from the Food and Drug Administration (FDA) for new drugs. The delays cost more than just money, too. Tens of thousands of Americans die because the drug that would save their lives is held up in endless bureaucratic red tape, even though it may already have been tested and approved and have a long history of use in other countries. Regulations can have fatal consequences.

15. Interstate Commerce Clause

The section of the Constitution that defines the "Enumerated Powers" of the federal government (Article I, Section 8) includes a clause that reads: "To regulate Commerce with foreign Nations, and among the several States, and with the Indian Tribes."

This clause is the source of much argument because of varying definitions of what constitutes commerce among the several states. A liberal interpretation of this has often prevailed, leading to the inclusion of any activity that *might* affect commerce between states, even if it does not now. Of course, that means that it includes virtually *every* conceivable human activity.

> *Regarding government boards or agencies, Hayek said: "By giving the government unlimited powers the most arbitrary rule can be made legal; and in this way a democracy [or republic] may set up the most complete despotism imaginable."*

If you grow beets in your garden and feed them to your family, it is possible that you are competing with beet growers in the neighboring states and it is also possible that your beets *might* some day be exported to other states, or that by eating them you are avoiding buying beets from another state, thus your beet garden can fall under government regulation. Or so the liberal argument goes.

Does that sound like an exaggeration? In 1942 a wheat farmer was ordered to pay a fine and to destroy wheat he had grown for use *on his own farm* (at a time when food was being rationed because of the war effort) because it *might* compete with wheat sold on the national market. The Supreme Court ruled in favor of the government regulators in Wickard v. Filburn.

This sort of overly-broad interpretation has been used to justify wide-reaching regulation of our personal and business activities that one would never suspect of being interstate commerce.

One other clause within Section 8 is often used to justify an über-liberal interpretation of the phrase "interstate commerce." It states that the Congress has the power to make laws that are "necessary and proper" to carry the powers listed (the Enumerated Powers) into execution.

Patrick Henry was suspicious of some of the broad language in The Constitution

This wording is obviously vague enough to lend itself to a wide variety of interpretations. There is no clear definition of what is meant by "necessary" or "proper" or who should arbitrate whether any thing is necessary or proper. It is no wonder that this is one of the clauses of the Constitution that Patrick Henry found particularly dangerous because it could easily be very broadly interpreted and thus lead to unlimited federal power. We can see today that Mr. Henry's concern was justified.

TO BE IN COMPLIANCE

As good law-abiding citizens, we certainly want to know that we are not violating any rules or regulations, don't we? So, how can we be sure?

The Federal Government must enforce its own rules. To do so, it has Law Enforcement Agencies. Because no one agency is able to keep up with all of the various existing and newly arriving rules and regulations, the government needs several agencies, each focusing on a defined subset of rules that it will enforce. So, how many Federal Law Enforcement Agencies are there? We counted 147 !

If it takes that many separate Law Enforcement Agencies with their staffs working full time to keep up with all the rules, how can any ordinary citizen be expected to keep up with them?

In the interest of space I will not list all of the federal police agencies here; but I will include a link in the back of the book so that you can satisfy your curiosity, if you wish. You might notice that many agencies that you would not suspect to be needing an armed police force of their own have one *or*

Even Social Security has its own armed police force

more law enforcement agencies within them. Social Security, Veterans Affairs—even Hoover Dam has its own police force.

Are you in compliance with all of the regulations? There is nobody in our government who can tell you the answer to that question—but *you* are expected to know.

16. Reforming Administrative Law

From the time our Constitution was drafted until it was ratified, a series of essays were written by several learned patriots arguing for or against ratification. These essays were published in newspapers and distributed among the people in all thirteen colonies so that they all participated in the debate. Essentially, the writings called "The Federalist Papers" argued for ratification, while those called "The Anti-Federalist papers" argued that the Constitution created a too-strong central government that would eventually use its powers to increase itself toward an inevitable tyranny.

> The Federalist Papers were written by James Madison, John Jay, and Alexander Hamilton, all using the pen name, "Publius." Publius was the name of a Roman who was instrumental in the establishment of a republican form of government.

In their much more recent essay titled "Reclaiming the Constitution," contemporary scholars Ted Cruz and Mario Loyola explain: "The fear of the Anti-Federalists now appears justified: If the power to regulate virtually all human activity is granted to the federal government in the simple phrase 'commerce among the several States,' what was left for the States or for the people?" Cruz, at the time of this writing, is a U.S. Senator representing Texas.

In an analysis of the Cruz-Loyola essay written for the Texas Public Policy Foundation (TPPF) Wesley A. Riddle observes:

> *"To the extent that both political parties have overseen and been complicit in the massive growth and rise in power of the federal government at the expense of States and individual rights, then both parties are responsible for undermining the Constitution and laying down hard pavement on the road to serfdom."*

Riddle, a Professor of Government at Central Texas College, is a former candidate for the US House of Representatives and a frequent contributor to academic journals and other publications. He may be contacted at **wes@wesriddle.com**.

It is comforting to know that there are at least a few good people in the public arena who understand the problem and will have the spine to fight for reform.

I believe that through appropriate reforms, we can reverse the damage done by excessive government intrusions into our business and personal lives without destroying the valid protections that the few useful regulations do provide. The reforms must install a mechanism for checking the powers of federal agencies much like our Constitution checked the powers of the three formal branches of government. They must also provide for the orderly demise of obsolete or misguided regulations once their usefulness has expired or they have been shown not to have been useful in the first place. (Consider the ethanol in your automobile fuel tank for example.)

Accomplishing these reforms will not be a simple task. There will be strong opposition from powerful forces; however, it is so necessary a task that it is well worth the risk and sacrifice that must be made.

While one could easily think of dozens of things that should be accommodated in the reforms, I will focus on three main items. I believe that if we can achieve these three, the positive effects upon our economy, our society, and our individual lives will be astounding.

- **Sunset All Rules and Regulations:** Every rule or regulation should include a "sunset clause" that requires it to be re-ratified or re-certified every so many years.

- **Require State Ratification:** Any rule or regulation that is beyond the Enumerated Powers of the federal government must be required to be ratified by the States, similarly to the way an amendment to the Constitution would have to be.

- **Term-Limit All Bureaucrats:** All administrators or heads of agencies and their subordinates at levels high enough to be able to affect policy decisions should be limited to a maximum number of years in office.

The Sunset Clause terms could vary based on the type of rule or regulation. For some, a one-year term might be advisable, for others a 20-year term, or anything in between. The term should be defined within the verbiage of the rule and there may be a different amount of time specified for the first term as compared to subsequent terms. Some regulations may have been a good idea at the time they were initiated; but because of changes over time, are no longer useful. In the military we had a term: "Overtaken by Events" (or "OBE") to describe a planned course of action that was no longer appropriate because of other events or alterations to a situation. The periodic review of every rule or regulation should include a determination whether it is OBE.

Some rules and regulations may have seemed like a good idea before being implemented; but later on are revealed to have been misguided. It is impossible for even the most well-intentioned and thoughtful planners to anticipate every effect that a proposed new rule might cause. It is not uncommon for them to notice unintended consequences of any action. These must be considered when reviewing any rule or regulation, as well. For example, if we increase the minimum wage to $10 per hour we might expect to improve the lot of the lowest-paid workers. However, if that action "prices them out of the market," the result might be much higher unemployment in just the group of people we intended to help.

Note: The minimum wage (which was a Progressive idea, remember) is advertised to combat poverty among workers and was originally promoted as opposing "sweat shops" in big cities; but it was promoted and supported by labor unions to make non-union labor more expensive—another example of corruption of the power to regulate to benefit a special-interest group for political purposes.

In general, I believe that any new rule or regulation should include an initial period that is rather brief—long enough to observe the actual effects of it; but short enough that we can expire it promptly if it does not seem to be working for the good. Then, subsequent reviews might be scheduled after longer intervals, if appropriate.

State Ratification should be accomplished by a vote with each State having one vote. Each State may decide how to administer their representation. Some might have their governor appoint a representative; some might have their legislature elect a representative. Each State could decide what they prefer; but each must provide one representative to the Ratification Congress, where the ratification voting will take place by an up-or-down vote.

Ratification of rules and regulations should not be quite as cumbersome as ratification of an amendment to the Constitution; but in instances in which the rule extends beyond the constitutional limits on federal authority, the States should have the power to accept or not accept each one. The Sunset Clause provision above gives the States the power to accept any new rule on a provisional basis, with the option to not re-ratify it in the future, thereby correcting past mistakes.

I am suggesting that each State choose one person as their representative to the Ratification Congress; but that each state may decide how they want to select that person. It is also possible that the Representative might require a small staff to help analyze the merits of each proposed new rule. Some might argue that this adds more "red tape" to our government processes; but I argue that any effort and expense that contributes to reining in the bureaucracy that is virtually uncontrolled now is well worthwhile. I believe that the Founders intended for any expansion of government to be difficult, rather than easy, to implement.

I will also suggest that any State that votes against ratification of any rule should be encouraged (or possibly required) to provide a brief explanation as to why. That might help the authors of these rules to understand the concerns of the States and to consider them in future works.

Term Limits for Bureaucrats are even more important than term limits for Congressmen and Senators. In fact, if we were to limit terms *only* for elected offices, we would actually be increasing the power of the already-too-powerful bureaucrats, who are not term-limited. Remember, we do have a way to fire elected officials — elections. We-The-People have no way to fire bureaucrats. If we limit terms for elected representatives we increase the number of newbies in our legislature. These novices would be highly dependent upon the much more experienced bureaucrats and unelected staffers for advice and direction.

Along with term limiting bureaucrats, we should also remove some of the obstacles to firing or laying off government employees. Government workers can perform poorly and misbehave grossly with impunity. They should be subject to the same sort of performance review that civilian workers are and, if they do not measure up, be subject to having their employment terminated. Nobody has a *right* to a government job!

I do not mean to imply that the three reforms I focused on are the *only* worthwhile reforms imaginable. Certainly not! Most of us should agree that a mechanism for verifying the validity of the "science" used to justify regulations and rules would be immensely beneficial. The massive "Global Warming Hoax" that has cost our country uncounted billions of dollars was based on what is known in the vernacular as "junk science." Some of it was probably simply the result of human error; but much of it was maliciously fabricated to support an Environmental Industry that sprang up to make a few people very wealthy and others very powerful.

> The Global Warming Hoax makes Bernie Madoff look like a small-time con man in comparison. I believe that the criminals responsible should be prosecuted and punished; but I am not very hopeful that we will ever see that happen.

Although many legitimate, credible scientists tried to point to the obvious flaws in the unproven theories that were passed off as the "consensus opinion of science," our bureaucracy continued to ignore any challenges and press forward with costly and damaging regulations that vastly increased their own powers.

EPA was the main agency supporting the Global Warming Hoax

Also, the problem we discussed earlier about the overly broad and ambiguous language of the "Interstate Commerce" and "Necessary and Proper" clauses within Article I of the Constitution should be cured by an Amendment clarifying what activities are included.

And, to be sure, the *automatic increases* in budgets for the federal government, almost all of which go to the Bureaucracy, must be stopped. The government utilizes a budgeting methodology that is called "baseline budgeting" which means that each year's budget is based on the prior year's budget, plus or minus adjustments. Because of inflation, it would seem proper to adjust the numerical dollar values up (or down, if appropriate) to maintain a level baseline; however, our government does not just use the actual inflation value for that adjustment, they bump it up by several points above the inflation value so that the typical adjustment to the baseline is about seven percent (7%) per year. That means that in a year that has "no budget increases" our budget actually increased by seven percent. That is how politicians argue that we have "cut the budget" if we have actually increased it by *only* six percent (6%). Thus, the Bureaucracy naturally expands at a rate considerably higher than the rate at which the overall economy expands and it grows even if the economy does not expand at all.

Finally, the entire system of Administrative Law Judges being appointed by the Executive Branch or by the agencies themselves should be looked at with an eye toward removing the bias in favor of the government. I explain a bit more about that in the discussion about the Administrative Procedures Act of 1946 in this book.

SHAM REFORM

Last year our President issued what, by its title, might sound like a move in the right direction. He issued: "Executive Order 13563 – Improving Regulation and Regulatory Review - January 18, 2011." It contains paragraph after paragraph of verbiage that paints a picture of a benevolent service organization that is our government bureaucracy.

At the end of the order, though, it says: "This order is not intended to, and does not, create any right or benefit, substantive or procedural, enforceable at law or in equity by any party against the United States, its departments, agencies, or entities, its officers, employees, or agents, or any other person. [signed] BARACK OBAMA." That is sort of like a lover promising to always be faithful—with his fingers crossed behind his back.

In other words, in the end it says nothing at all, just like a campaign speech.

INSIDE BASEBALL

You and I are not the first persons to recognize that reform of Administrative Law is needed. In the decades since the New Deal there have been others. But the issue has an "inside baseball" quality that has made it difficult to arouse much enthusiasm for it among the general public. Although many people are incensed by one regulation or another, few people make the connection back to the actual source of the problem.

To stick with the baseball analogy, if you were to propose that the National League adopt the Designated Hitter Rule you would get lots of strong opinions and heated debate from fans for or against the proposal. It would be a very animated argument with lots of people taking a position and a lot of passion and involvement.

If you were to propose that MLB require that baseball bats made of maple wood should have a two millimeter larger minimum diameter at their narrowest point to reduce broken bats, you would probably get an unenthusiastic "ho-hum" response from fans (not from players, though).

But the first proposal merely has the potential to affect the outcome of some games while the second has the potential to prevent serious injuries or even deaths from heavy, pointed missiles flying at high speed across the infield or into the stands.

So it is with the issue of reforming Administrative Law. The passions of the People are easily captured by issues that have far less impact on our nation; but whose impact is more visible. For example, imposing term limits on Senators and Representatives is a very popular proposal. I agree with term limits; but I think that it is far more important to *first* impose term limits on every officer in the Bureaucracy who is at a level high enough to influence policy. After all, there already is a way to get bad politicians out of office — elections. There is virtually no way for us to get bad bureaucrats out of office.

> Note: There is precedent for term limiting bureaucrats. After J. Edgar Hoover died, thus terminating his 48-year reign as Director of the FBI, Congress imposed a ten-year term limit on that office so as to prevent anyone else from ever achieving the level of power Hoover had. Hoover was arguably the most powerful man in Washington, Senators and even Presidents notwithstanding.

Returning momentarily to the national pastime, if a sufficient number of serious and dramatic incidents were to result from broken maple bats, I imagine that the issue of strengthening the bats would become much more popular all of a sudden. In this book I try to describe a few of the many thousands of really offensive regulations that have been imposed on us in hopes that readers might be aroused to passion about the issue of reform.

> Baseball again: There already have been incidents and injuries resulting from broken maple bats and there have been many, many near misses that might have been very serious or even fatal. It just has not reached the threshold at which it triggers the level of support for a remedy that is needed.

REINS ACT

There is a reform bill being proposed by some in Congress called the "Regulations from the Executive in Need of Scrutiny" (REINS) Act. The bill is called H.R. 10 in the House and S. 299 in the Senate. I do not believe that it is an effective or useful bill for several reasons. In fact, I think it would do more harm than good. Why? Let me explain.

The bill attempts to attack the problems I describe in this book by requiring that all regulations that are considered "major" must be voted on by the House of Representatives and the Senate and approved by the President. This is intended to make our Federal Government elected officials accountable for all regulations passed. Any regulations that have an economic effect of $100 million or more are defined, for this bill, as being "major".

There are several problems with this idea.

First, who decides how much economic impact any given bill will have? Our government is notoriously inept at projecting costs. The Affordable Healthcare bill was projected to have a cost of $800 billion two years ago. Our government has revised that to more than double this year. Government estimates of economic impact are not very reliable. Even if they could accurately project the impact for the next year, changes that occur in demographics, technology, and world affairs have a tendency to multiply costs unexpectedly.

Second, our Constitution does not provide that the Federal Government may do whatever it wishes so long as the cost is below some threshold. Economic impact is not my paramount concern, the loss of our liberty is.

Third, even if regulators could not avoid projecting the cost of some regulation from being over the threshold, it would not be difficult for them to divide the regulation into many smaller regulations that each fall below the threshold amount and thus accomplish the same thing. Figures don't lie; but liars do figure.

Fourth, the function of the Bureaucracy is to deal with the details of laws passed by the Legislature. That is because the workload of researching every issue to determine what regulation is appropriate would be far too much for 435 Representatives or 100 Senators to micro-manage. I said earlier that I agree that there is a legitimate purpose for the Bureaucracy. Also, the imposition of Federal regulations is actually an appropriation of State Powers. That is why the solution I propose in this book establishes a Ratification Congress that represents the 50 States. The voice of the States was essentially muted in the Federal Government a century ago. My proposal at least partially restores it.

Finally, the passage of such a bill would give the false impression that the problem has been fixed. The REINS Act would not accomplish any real reform; but it would prevent genuine reforms from being made. We actually already do have some experience with the effect of a "reform" that does not really reform Administrative Law. We can start by looking back to 1946.

17. Administrative Procedures Act – 1946

The first attempt at reforming Administrative Law and the Bureaucracy started just a few years after FDR initiated his New Deal and began creating agencies with sweeping powers. Lawmakers spent a decade working on a solution to the problem of a Fourth Branch of government having been created with virtually no restrictions upon it. In 1946 they passed the Administrative Procedures Act (APA) that set forth the methods and procedures that government agencies were to follow in making rules and regulations and enforcing them.

> Note: the notion that a Fourth Branch of government had been established that was not sanctioned by the Constitution did not originate with me. It was being discussed as early as the 1930's.

Unfortunately, it contained a lot of toothless verbiage with few penalties for agencies violating the rules and plenty of exemptions. It did establish standard operating procedures and protocols. It did create a formal method for adjudicating disputes. It may have created the *illusion* of a reform; but it did not really reform what needed to be reformed, as we can easily see by the way the Bureaucracy has since grown and expanded to reach to control even the smallest details of our lives, and by the way agencies routinely act far outside their original jurisdictions.

Since then there have been committees and task forces studying the problem; but with little or no substantive results.

The fact is that too few Americans, even many who are politically savvy in many other ways, understand the problem and thus the level of interest has not been high enough to propel genuine reform.

Additionally, over half our population now relies on government for some or all of their monthly income. Social Security, Welfare, Food Stamps, Disability, government salary, government pension, subsidies, et cetera, et cetera, all make the recipients reluctant to fight the hand that feeds them and willing to overlook the loss of their own liberty in exchange for the continuation of their benefit.

We need a *real* reform. We need to bring the Fourth Branch under control the way our Founders intended all of our federal government should be.

In the national debate that preceded ratification of our Constitution, Patrick Henry (an Anti-Federalist) warned that they were creating a central government that was too strong and would break loose of the bonds that the Constitution placed upon it. Alexander Hamilton (a Federalist) argued that it would not. Henry was apparently right. Now *we* must make Hamilton right in order to preserve our republic.

ADMINISTRATIVE LAW JUDGES

Special judges adjudicate disputes between individuals and agencies

A part of the "reform" that the 1946 APA installed was a mechanism for adjudicating disputes between us and the federal agencies. Prior to APA the agencies themselves acted as judges for cases against themselves. Special judges, called Administrative Law Judges, now handle such cases. These judges are appointed, not elected, and they must pass a qualifying test of knowledge (hence, they are "experts") about Administrative Law. There are Administrative Law judges at the federal level and for every state, with many similarities among them.

First, these judges and their courts are within the Executive Branch, not the Judicial Branch of government. They are appointed by either political officials in the Executive Branch, persons appointed by those politicians, or by the agencies themselves, making them very likely to be sympathetic to the interests of the Bureaucracy over the interests of the individuals and organizations that are being regulated, or of the Constitution. Even if we assume that a judge has the personal integrity to avoid any relationships with the agency whose cases he handles, we must assume that when the agency chose to appoint him, it sought a person who would have a favorable inclination toward their agency.

Generally, if an individual sues an agency, he/she must exhaust *all avenues* of mediation and trial before an Administrative Law Judge and any subsequent appeals in Administrative Law Courts before being allowed to bring the case to any federal or state court. That can be so long and expensive a process that most people will just give up—particularly when they realize that they are facing a judge who was *selected and appointed by* the agency they are suing.

Note: The Founders went to great lengths to establish a Separation of Powers. That meant that the branch of government that made laws was entirely separated from the branch that enforced those laws and also from the one that adjudicated cases based on those laws. This separation was fundamental to their design. In fact, Thomas Jefferson once said that the *definition of tyranny* was the absence of the Separation of Powers and James Madison agreed. When FDR created this Fourth Branch, it was given the powers to make rules, enforce those rules, and to adjudicate cases involving those rules. That was a clear violation of a fundamental principle of our American form of government—a principle so fundamental, in fact, that the Federalist, Madison, and the Anti-Federalist, Jefferson, agreed completely on it. The APA did not correct this problem, it merely masked it by establishing what appears to be a judiciary, the Administrative Court, but is actually merely another agency within the agency whose rules it is dealing with. In other words, instead of correcting the problem it added an official- and proper-looking protocol. Lipstick on the pig?

"The accumulation of all powers, legislative, executive, and judiciary, in the same hands, whether of one, a few, or many, and whether hereditary, selfappointed, or elective, may justly be pronounced the very definition of tyranny." – James Madison, Federalist #47

Note: A fundamental principle of Progressivism was that the Separation of Powers was an impediment to "efficient" government that should be flexible enough to adjust to the changing needs of the country, and that it hampered the work of the "experts" who should rightfully be in control. Their argument was that a body having parts that were fighting against one another could not survive. This argument presumes that the nature of government is more similar to a biological entity than to a societal construct. It is a clever distortion that will sway many minds too lazy to examine the assumptions and reasoning behind it.

Administrative Law Courts and the judges who officiate in them were established in 1946 by the APA. Originally the judges were required to "possess a professional license to practice law and be authorized to practice law". That gave at least the appearance of propriety. In 2008, according to the Office of Personnel Management (OPM), they suspended that requirement. So, I suppose, the only remaining requirement to be an Administrative Law Judge is the right political or bureaucratic connections.

18. State & Local Bureaucracies

In this book I am addressing only the Federal Bureaucracy. I do acknowledge that each state has its own bureaucracy and that they have some of the same shortcomings. Since most states more or less structure their bureaucracies after the federal model, we can expect that when we have reformed the central system, the states will follow suit. In fact, the Federal Government does provide an actual model (Model State Administrative Procedure Act [MSAPA]) that it encourages states to follow.

State regulating agencies operate in a different legal environment since the Constitution specifically limits the powers of the central government with the express intent of leaving most powers to the states, or to the people themselves. Many forms of regulation that would be unconstitutional for the federal government would be perfectly legal for the states themselves. That does not imply that all state regulations are beneficial, though.

One premise that I certainly agree with is that the closer to the people that a governing body is, the better it is likely to govern. Thus, I would much prefer to have, say, the Texas Commission on Environmental Quality (TCEQ) oversee environmental issues for the state of Texas than for the federal EPA to do it. TCEQ may or may not be better qualified; but they would be much more responsive to the desires and needs of Texas and Texans than the federal agency would be. Because they would be closer to the people they are affecting, the people could more easily replace bad commissioners by putting pressure on their local representatives. Moving regulation from the federal to the state level does not solve every problem; but it does solve some and it makes others easier to solve moving forward.

Some matters would be better handled at an even lower level. Education is a prime example. The federal Department of Education (ED) was established to ostensibly improve education in the US so that we could better compete with other countries whose youth were surpassing us in math and language education and test scores. Its mission was to make our youth competitive with those of other countries.

According to a recent 3-year study done by the Organisation for Economic Co-operation and Development (OECD, an international organization) of 34 OECD countries, American 15-year-olds ranked 14th in reading, 17th in science, and 25th in mathematics. This is in spite of the fact that the US expenditure per student is one of the highest in the world at over $6,000/year. In fact, in some of the worst performing areas of the nation, spending is far higher per student. In 2009 The District of Columbia spent over $19,600 per student and produced some of the worst scores in the country.

Since its inception in 1979, we can track a nearly continuous decline in the performance of our students as compared to other countries' students. The ED is mainly focused on anti-discrimination and political correctness issues — indoctrination instead of education. From the start it was strongly supported by the National Education Association (NEA), a very left-wing and highly politicized union of teachers that is often blamed for our rapid decline in academic quality and focus on political thought control in our public schools.

Some go so far as to claim that the NEA and the ED collaborate to *lower* academic education standards because a "dumbed-down," dependent population is easier for a government to manipulate and control. I have to confess that I see a lot of evidence to support that theory.

Since the ED has no purpose that is useful to the population, it ought to be eliminated altogether. But every state already has is own Department of Education or Education Department. Education is best managed from the lowest possible level. Even the state-level departments have too much control from too remote a level. Students who are taught in private schools consistently outperform public school students. A part of the reason is because the private schools are managed locally, not from afar. To carry that even further, home schooled students usually also out perform public school students, sometimes even private school students. That is because their education decisions are being made from the lowest possible level, their parents. Nobody knows the students better than their parents and nobody cares about them more than their parents do.

I would hope that once we have implemented reform to diminish government regulation and control at the highest level, the spirit of that reform would trickle down to states and even to cities. After all, we would not want some municipal government to try to tell us what size soft drink we are allowed to buy or some other ridiculous micro-management of our personal lives, would we?

> A vivid illustration of how the power to regulate or to license can easily be corrupted for political ends is apparent in the recent refusals of some large city mayors to issue business licenses to Chick-fil-A stores because of the company's stance on gay marriage. It seems that you must agree with these mayors' politics if you wish to do business in their cities. Although this is at a municipal level, not the federal level, it readily demonstrates how the power to license and regulate can so easily be politicized and misused.

To give you an idea of how state governments can add immense weight to the burden already placed upon us by the federal government, if you wish to live and do business in California, you might want to check to see that you are not running afoul of any state offices, agencies, bureaus, or boards. Here is a checklist to help you:

- ☐ California Academic Performance Index (API)
- ☐ California Access for Infants and Mothers
- ☐ California Acupuncture Board
- ☐ California Administrative Office of the Courts
- ☐ California Adoptions Branch
- ☐ California African American Museum
- ☐ California Agricultural Export Program
- ☐ California Agricultural Labor Relations Board
- ☐ California Agricultural Statistics Service
- ☐ California Air Resources Board (CARB)
- ☐ California Allocation Board
- ☐ California Alternative Energy and Advanced Transportation Financing Authority
- ☐ California Animal Health and Food Safety Services
- ☐ California Anti-Terrorism Information Center
- ☐ California Apprenticeship Council
- ☐ California Arbitration Certification Program
- ☐ California Architects Board
- ☐ California Area VI Developmental Disabilities Board

- ☐ California Arts Council
- ☐ California Asian Pacific Islander Legislative Caucus
- ☐ California Assembly Democratic Caucus
- ☐ California Assembly Republican Caucus
- ☐ California Athletic Commission
- ☐ California Attorney General
- ☐ California Bay Conservation and Development Commission
- ☐ California Bay-Delta Authority
- ☐ California Bay-Delta Office
- ☐ California Bio Diversity Council
- ☐ California Board for Geologists and Geophysicists
- ☐ California Board for Professional Engineers and Land Surveyors
- ☐ California Board of Accountancy
- ☐ California Board of Barbering and Cosmetology
- ☐ California Board of Behavioral Sciences
- ☐ California Board of Chiropractic Examiners
- ☐ California Board of Equalization (BOE)
- ☐ California Board of Forestry and Fire Protection
- ☐ California Board of Guide Dogs for the Blind
- ☐ California Board of Occupational Therapy
- ☐ California Board of Optometry
- ☐ California Board of Pharmacy
- ☐ California Board of Podiatric Medicine
- ☐ California Board of Prison Terms
- ☐ California Board of Psychology
- ☐ California Board of Registered Nursing
- ☐ California Board of Trustees
- ☐ California Board of Vocational Nursing and Psychiatric Technicians
- ☐ California Braille and Talking Book Library
- ☐ California Building Standards Commission
- ☐ California Bureau for Private Post Secondary and Vocational Education
- ☐ California Bureau of Automotive Repair
- ☐ California Bureau of Electronic and Appliance Repair
- ☐ California Bureau of Home Furnishings and Thermal Insulation
- ☐ California Bureau of Naturopathic Medicine
- ☐ California Bureau of Security and Investigative Services
- ☐ California Bureau of State Audits
- ☐ California Business Agency
- ☐ California Business Investment Services (CalBIS)
- ☐ California Business Permit Information (CalGOLD)
- ☐ California Business Portal
- ☐ California Business, Transportation and Housing Agency
- ☐ California Cal Grants
- ☐ California CalJOBS
- ☐ California Cal-Learn Program
- ☐ California CalVet Home Loan Program
- ☐ California Career Resource Network
- ☐ California Cemetery and Funeral Bureau
- ☐ California Center for Analytical Chemistry
- ☐ California Center for Distributed Learning
- ☐ California Center for Teaching Careers (Teach California)
- ☐ California Chancellors Office
- ☐ California Charter Schools
- ☐ California Children and Families Commission
- ☐ California Children and Family Services Division
- ☐ California Citizens Compensation Commission

- ☐ California Civil Rights Bureau
- ☐ California Coastal Commission
- ☐ California Coastal Conservancy
- ☐ California Code of Regulations
- ☐ California Collaborative Projects with UC Davis
- ☐ California Commission for Jobs and Economic Growth
- ☐ California Commission on Aging
- ☐ California Commission on Health and Safety and Workers Compensation
- ☐ California Commission on Judicial Performance
- ☐ California Commission on State Mandates
- ☐ California Commission on Status of Women
- ☐ California Commission on Teacher Credentialing
- ☐ California Commission on the Status of Women
- ☐ California Committee on Dental Auxiliaries
- ☐ California Community Colleges Chancellors Office, Junior Colleges
- ☐ California Community Colleges Chancellors Office
- ☐ California Complaint Mediation Program
- ☐ California Conservation Corps
- ☐ California Constitution Revision Commission
- ☐ California Consumer Hotline
- ☐ California Consumer Information Center
- ☐ California Consumer Information
- ☐ California Consumer Services Division
- ☐ California Consumers and Families Agency
- ☐ California Contractors State License Board
- ☐ California Corrections Standards Authority
- ☐ California Council for the Humanities
- ☐ California Council on Criminal Justice
- ☐ California Council on Developmental Disabilities
- ☐ California Court Reporters Board
- ☐ California Courts of Appeal
- ☐ California Crime and Violence Prevention Center
- ☐ California Criminal Justice Statistics Center
- ☐ California Criminalist Institute Forensic Library
- ☐ California CSGnet Network Management
- ☐ California Cultural and Historical Endowment
- ☐ California Cultural Resources Division
- ☐ California Curriculum and Instructional Leadership Branch
- ☐ California Data Exchange Center
- ☐ California Data Management Division
- ☐ California Debt and Investment Advisory Commission
- ☐ California Delta Protection Commission
- ☐ California Democratic Caucus
- ☐ California Demographic Research Unit
- ☐ California Dental Auxiliaries
- ☐ California Department of Aging
- ☐ California Department of Alcohol and Drug Programs
- ☐ California Department of Alcoholic Beverage Control Appeals Board
- ☐ California Department of Alcoholic Beverage Control
- ☐ California Department of Boating and Waterways (Cal Boating)
- ☐ California Department of Child Support Services (CDCSS)
- ☐ California Department of Community Services and Development
- ☐ California Department of Conservation
- ☐ California Department of Consumer Affairs
- ☐ California Department of Corporations
- ☐ California Department of Corrections and Rehabilitation

- ☐ California Department of Developmental Services
- ☐ California Department of Education
- ☐ California Department of Fair Employment and Housing
- ☐ California Department of Finance
- ☐ California Department of Financial Institutions
- ☐ California Department of Fish and Game
- ☐ California Department of Food and Agriculture
- ☐ California Department of Forestry and Fire Protection (CDF)
- ☐ California Department of General Services
- ☐ California Department of General Services, Office of State Publishing
- ☐ California Department of Health Care Services
- ☐ California Department of Housing and Community Development
- ☐ California Department of Industrial Relations (DIR)
- ☐ California Department of Insurance
- ☐ California Department of Justice Firearms Division
- ☐ California Department of Justice Opinion Unit
- ☐ California Department of Justice, Consumer Information, Public Inquiry Unit
- ☐ California Department of Justice
- ☐ California Department of Managed Health Care
- ☐ California Department of Mental Health
- ☐ California Department of Motor Vehicles (DMV)
- ☐ California Department of Personnel Administration
- ☐ California Department of Pesticide Regulation
- ☐ California Department of Public Health
- ☐ California Department of Real Estate
- ☐ California Department of Rehabilitation
- ☐ California Department of Social Services Adoptions Branch
- ☐ California Department of Social Services
- ☐ California Department of Technology Services Training Center (DTSTC)
- ☐ California Department of Technology Services (DTS)
- ☐ California Department of Toxic Substances Control
- ☐ California Department of Transportation (Caltrans)
- ☐ California Department of Veterans Affairs (CalVets)
- ☐ California Department of Water Resources
- ☐ California Departmento de Vehiculos Motorizados
- ☐ California Digital Library
- ☐ California Disabled Veteran Business Enterprise Certification Program
- ☐ California Division of Apprenticeship Standards
- ☐ California Division of Codes and Standards
- ☐ California Division of Communicable Disease Control
- ☐ California Division of Engineering
- ☐ California Division of Environmental and Occupational Disease Control
- ☐ California Division of Gambling Control
- ☐ California Division of Housing Policy Development
- ☐ California Division of Labor Standards Enforcement
- ☐ California Division of Labor Statistics and Research
- ☐ California Division of Land and Right of Way
- ☐ California Division of Land Resource Protection
- ☐ California Division of Law Enforcement General Library
- ☐ California Division of Measurement Standards
- ☐ California Division of Mines and Geology
- ☐ California Division of Occupational Safety and Health (Cal/OSHA)
- ☐ California Division of Oil, Gas and Geothermal Resources
- ☐ California Division of Planning and Local Assistance
- ☐ California Division of Recycling
- ☐ California Division of Safety of Dams

- ☐ California Division of the State Architect
- ☐ California Division of Tourism
- ☐ California Division of Workers Compensation Medical Unit
- ☐ California Division of Workers Compensation
- ☐ California Economic Assistance, Business and Community Resources
- ☐ California Economic Strategy Panel
- ☐ California Education and Training Agency
- ☐ California Education Audit Appeals Panel
- ☐ California Educational Facilities Authority
- ☐ California Elections Division
- ☐ California Electricity Oversight Board
- ☐ California Emergency Management Agency
- ☐ California Emergency Medical Services Authority
- ☐ California Employment Development Department (EDD)
- ☐ California Employment Information State Jobs
- ☐ California Employment Training Panel
- ☐ California Energy Commission
- ☐ California Environment and Natural Resources Agency
- ☐ California Environmental Protection Agency (Cal/EPA)
- ☐ California Environmental Resources Evaluation System (CERES)
- ☐ California Executive Office
- ☐ California Export Laboratory Services
- ☐ California Exposition and State Fair(Cal Expo)
- ☐ California Fair Political Practices Commission
- ☐ California Fairs and Expositions Division
- ☐ California Film Commission
- ☐ California Fire and Resource Assessment Program
- ☐ California Firearms Division
- ☐ California Fiscal Services
- ☐ California Fish and Game Commission
- ☐ California Fisheries Program Branch
- ☐ California Floodplain Management
- ☐ California Foster Youth Help
- ☐ California Franchise Tax Board (FTB)
- ☐ California Fraud Division
- ☐ California Gambling Control Commission
- ☐ California Geographic Information Systems Council (GIS)
- ☐ California Geological Survey
- ☐ California Government Claims and Victim Compensation Board
- ☐ California Governors Committee for Employment of Disabled Persons
- ☐ California Governors Mentoring Partnership
- ☐ California Governors Office of Emergency Services
- ☐ California Governors Office of Homeland Security
- ☐ California Governors Office of Planning and Research
- ☐ California Governors Office
- ☐ California Grant and Enterprise Zone Programs HCD Loan
- ☐ California Health and Human Services Agency
- ☐ California Health and Safety Agency
- ☐ California Healthy Families Program
- ☐ California Hearing Aid Dispensers Bureau
- ☐ California High-Speed Rail Authority
- ☐ California Highway Patrol (CHP)
- ☐ California History and Culture Agency
- ☐ California Horse Racing Board
- ☐ California Housing Finance Agency
- ☐ California Indoor Air Quality Program

- ☐ California Industrial Development Financing Advisory Commission
- ☐ California Industrial Welfare Commission
- ☐ California InFoPeople
- ☐ California Information Center for the Environment
- ☐ California Infrastructure and Economic Development Bank (I-Bank)
- ☐ California Inspection Services
- ☐ California Institute for County Government
- ☐ California Institute for Education Reform
- ☐ California Integrated Waste Management Board
- ☐ California Interagency Ecological Program
- ☐ California Job Service
- ☐ California Junta Estatal de Personal
- ☐ California Labor and Employment Agency
- ☐ California Labor and Workforce Development Agency
- ☐ California Labor Market Information Division
- ☐ California Land Use Planning Information Network (LUPIN)
- ☐ California Lands Commission
- ☐ California Landscape Architects Technical Committee
- ☐ California Latino Legislative Caucus
- ☐ California Law Enforcement Branch
- ☐ California Law Enforcement General Library
- ☐ California Law Revision Commission
- ☐ California Legislative Analyst's Office
- ☐ California Legislative Black Caucus
- ☐ California Legislative Counsel
- ☐ California Legislative Division
- ☐ California Legislative Information
- ☐ California Legislative Lesbian, Gay, Bisexual, and Transgender (LGBT) Caucus
- ☐ California Legislature Internet Caucus
- ☐ California Library Development Services
- ☐ California License and Revenue Branch
- ☐ California Major Risk Medical Insurance Program
- ☐ California Managed Risk Medical Insurance Board
- ☐ California Maritime Academy
- ☐ California Marketing Services
- ☐ California Measurement Standards
- ☐ California Medical Assistance Commission
- ☐ California Medical Care Services
- ☐ California Military Department
- ☐ California Mining and Geology Board
- ☐ California Museum for History, Women, and the Arts
- ☐ California Museum Resource Center
- ☐ California National Guard
- ☐ California Native American Heritage Commission
- ☐ California Natural Community Conservation Planning Program
- ☐ California New Motor Vehicle Board
- ☐ California Nursing Home Administrator Program
- ☐ California Occupational Safety and Health Appeals Board
- ☐ California Occupational Safety and Health Standards Board
- ☐ California Ocean Resources Management Program
- ☐ California Office of Administrative Hearings
- ☐ California Office of Administrative Law
- ☐ California Office of AIDS
- ☐ California Office of Binational Border Health
- ☐ California Office of Child Abuse Prevention
- ☐ California Office of Deaf Access

114

- California Office of Emergency Services (OES)
- California Office of Environmental Health Hazard Assessment
- California Office of Fiscal Services
- California Office of Fleet Administration
- California Office of Health Insurance Portability and Accountability Act (HIPAA) Implementation (CalOHI)
- California Office of Historic Preservation
- California Office of Homeland Security
- California Office of Human Resources
- California Office of Legal Services
- California Office of Legislation
- California Office of Lieutenant Governor
- California Office of Military and Aerospace Support
- California Office of Mine Reclamation
- California Office of Natural Resource Education
- California Office of Privacy Protection
- California Office of Public School Construction
- California Office of Real Estate Appraisers
- California Office of Risk and Insurance Management
- California Office of Services to the Blind
- California Office of Spill Prevention and Response
- California Office of State Publishing (OSP)
- California Office of Statewide Health Planning and Development
- California Office of Systems Integration
- California Office of the Inspector General
- California Office of the Ombudsman
- California Office of the Patient Advocate
- California Office of the President
- California Office of the Secretary for Education
- California Office of the State Fire Marshal
- California Office of the State Public Defender
- California Office of Traffic Safety
- California Office of Vital Records
- California Online Directory
- California Operations Control Office
- California Opinion Unit
- California Outreach and Technical Assistance Network (OTAN)
- California Park and Recreation Commission
- California Peace Officer Standards and Training (POST)
- California Performance Review (CPR)
- California Permit Information for Business (CalGOLD)
- California Physical Therapy Board
- California Physician Assistant Committee
- California Plant Health and Pest Prevention Services
- California Policy and Evaluation Division
- California Political Reform Division
- California Pollution Control Financing Authority
- California Polytechnic State University, San Luis Obispo
- California Postsecondary Education Commission
- California Prevention Services
- California Primary Care and Family Health
- California Prison Industry Authority
- California Procurement Division
- California Public Employees Retirement System (CalPERS)
- California Public Employment Relations Board (PERB)
- California Public Utilities Commission (PUC)

- ☐ California Real Estate Services Division
- ☐ California Refugee Programs Branch
- ☐ California Regional Water Quality Control Boards
- ☐ California Registered Veterinary Technician Committee
- ☐ California Registrar of Charitable Trusts
- ☐ California Republican Caucus
- ☐ California Research and Development Division
- ☐ California Research Bureau
- ☐ California Resources Agency
- ☐ California Respiratory Care Board
- ☐ California Rivers Assessment
- ☐ California Rural Health Policy Council
- ☐ California Safe Schools
- ☐ California San Francisco Bay Conservation and Development Commission
- ☐ California San Gabriel and Lower Los Angeles Rivers and Mountains Conservancy
- ☐ California San Joaquin River Conservancy
- ☐ California School to Career
- ☐ California Science Center
- ☐ California Scripps Institution of Oceanography
- ☐ California Secretary of State Business Portal
- ☐ California Secretary of State
- ☐ California Seismic Safety Commission
- ☐ California Self Insurance Plans (SIP)
- ☐ California Senate Office of Research
- ☐ California Small Business and Disabled Veteran Business Enterprise Certification Program
- ☐ California Small Business Development Center Program
- ☐ California Smart Growth Caucus
- ☐ California Smog Check Information Center
- ☐ California Spatial Information Library
- ☐ California Special Education Division
- ☐ California Speech-Language Pathology and Audiology Board
- ☐ California Standardized Testing and Reporting (STAR)
- ☐ California Standards and Assessment Division
- ☐ California State Administrative Manual (SAM)
- ☐ California State Allocation Board
- ☐ California State and Consumer Services Agency
- ☐ California State Architect
- ☐ California State Archives
- ☐ California State Assembly
- ☐ California State Association of Counties (CSAC)
- ☐ California State Board of Education
- ☐ California State Board of Food and Agriculture
- ☐ California Office of the Chief Information Officer (OCIO)
- ☐ California State Children's Trust Fund
- ☐ California State Compensation Insurance Fund
- ☐ California State Contracts Register Program
- ☐ California State Contracts Register
- ☐ California State Controller
- ☐ California State Council on Developmental Disabilities (SCDD)
- ☐ California State Disability Insurance (SDI)
- ☐ California State Fair (Cal Expo)
- ☐ California State Jobs Employment Information
- ☐ California State Lands Commission
- ☐ California State Legislative Portal

- ☐ California State Legislature
- ☐ California State Library Catalog
- ☐ California State Library Services Bureau
- ☐ California State Library
- ☐ California State Lottery
- ☐ California State Mediation and Conciliation Service
- ☐ California State Mining and Geology Board
- ☐ California State Park and Recreation Commission
- ☐ California State Parks
- ☐ California State Personnel Board
- ☐ California State Polytechnic University, Pomona
- ☐ California State Railroad Museum
- ☐ California State Science Fair
- ☐ California State Senate
- ☐ California State Summer School for Mathematics and Science (COSMOS)
- ☐ California State Summer School for the Arts
- ☐ California State Superintendent of Public Instruction
- ☐ California State Teachers Retirement System (CalSTRS)
- ☐ California State Treasurer
- ☐ California State University Center for Distributed Learning
- ☐ California State University, Bakersfield
- ☐ California State University, Channel Islands
- ☐ California State University, Chico
- ☐ California State University, Dominguez Hills
- ☐ California State University, East Bay
- ☐ California State University, Fresno
- ☐ California State University, Fullerton
- ☐ California State University, Long Beach
- ☐ California State University, Los Angeles
- ☐ California State University, Monterey Bay
- ☐ California State University, Northridge
- ☐ California State University, Sacramento
- ☐ California State University, San Bernardino
- ☐ California State University, San Marcos
- ☐ California State University, Stanislaus
- ☐ California State University (CSU)
- ☐ California State Water Project Analysis Office
- ☐ California State Water Project
- ☐ California State Water Resources Control Board
- ☐ California Structural Pest Control Board
- ☐ California Student Aid Commission
- ☐ California Superintendent of Public Instruction
- ☐ California Superior Courts
- ☐ California Tahoe Conservancy
- ☐ California Task Force on Culturally and Linguistically Competent Physicians and Dentists
- ☐ California Tax Information Center
- ☐ California Technology and Administration Branch Finance
- ☐ California Telecommunications Division
- ☐ California Telephone Medical Advice Services (TAMS)
- ☐ California Transportation Commission
- ☐ California Travel and Transportation Agency
- ☐ California Unclaimed Property Program
- ☐ California Unemployment Insurance Appeals Board
- ☐ California Unemployment Insurance Program
- ☐ California Uniform Construction Cost Accounting Commission

- ☐ California Veterans Board
- ☐ California Veterans Memorial
- ☐ California Veterinary Medical Board and Registered Veterinary Technician Examining Committee
- ☐ California Veterinary Medical Board
- ☐ California Victim Compensation and Government Claims Board
- ☐ California Volunteers
- ☐ California Voter Registration
- ☐ California Water Commission
- ☐ California Water Environment Association (COWPEA)
- ☐ California Water Resources Control Board
- ☐ California Welfare to Work Division
- ☐ California Wetlands Information System
- ☐ California Wildlife and Habitat Data Analysis Branch
- ☐ California Wildlife Conservation Board
- ☐ California Wildlife Programs Branch
- ☐ California Work Opportunity and Responsibility to Kids (CalWORKs)
- ☐ California Workers Compensation Appeals Board
- ☐ California Workforce and Labor Development Agency
- ☐ California Workforce Investment Board
- ☐ California Youth Authority (CYA)
- ☐ Central Valley Flood Protection Board
- ☐ Center for California Studies
- ☐ Colorado River Board of California
- ☐ Counting California
- ☐ Dental Board of California
- ☐ Health Insurance Plan of California (PacAdvantage)
- ☐ Humboldt State University
- ☐ Jobs with the State of California
- ☐ Judicial Council of California
- ☐ Learn California
- ☐ Library of California
- ☐ Lieutenant Governors Commission for One California
- ☐ Little Hoover Commission (on California State Government Organization and Economy)
- ☐ Medical Board of California
- ☐ Medi-Cal
- ☐ Osteopathic Medical Board of California
- ☐ Physical Therapy Board of California
- ☐ Regents of the University of California
- ☐ San Diego State University
- ☐ San Francisco State University
- ☐ San Jose State University
- ☐ Santa Monica Mountains Conservancy
- ☐ State Bar of California
- ☐ Supreme Court of California
- ☐ University of California
- ☐ University of California, Berkeley
- ☐ University of California, Davis
- ☐ University of California, Hastings College of the Law
- ☐ University of California, Irvine
- ☐ University of California, Los Angeles
- ☐ University of California, Merced
- ☐ University of California, Riverside
- ☐ University of California, San Diego
- ☐ University of California, San Francisco

- ☐ University of California, Santa Barbara
- ☐ University of California, Santa Cruz
- ☐ Veterans Home of California

Please excuse me for wasting so much space with this list; but I believe that it illustrates a point.

Also, don't be fooled by the name of an agency. The name does not always indicate what it does at all. In Texas, you do not need to worry about the Texas Railroad Commission (TxRRC) if you are running a railroad; but you definitely do if you want to drill for oil or gas. In spite of its name, it has nothing to do with railroads—it regulates energy exploration and gas pipelines.

> Note: TxRRC is one of the few regulatory agencies in any state run by elected, rather than appointed, commissioners—a three-person panel. That makes the agency somewhat more answerable to the public for its actions. Of the three commissioners, one, Barry Smitherman, Committee Chairman, has publicly endorsed our mission to reform Administrative Law, and another has already told Mr. Smitherman that he also supports our goals. I doubt that many *appointed* officials will share that position.

Additionally, I can assure you that many business owners have found that it is actually not possible to be compliant with all the regulations because the rules of one agency can be in direct conflict with the rules of another. For instance, a former operator of a day care facility for children reported being required by the Fire Marshall to have a fire extinguisher hung on the wall of every room within reach of occupants while the Department of Health and Human Services required that there be no heavy objects hung on the walls. Numerous other examples of contradictory regulations can be found.

A recent news story reports about entrepreneurial Nathan Duszynski, age 13, having his business shut down because of regulations designed to protect certain local businesses from competition. Nathan had a license to sell hot dogs from the cart he purchased with his own money that he had earned mowing lawns. He worked and started his business to assist his parents, both of whom are disabled. Regulations pushed by local restaurants in his town of Holland, Michigan and by the teachers' union put him out of business. That left Nathan and his parents unable to afford housing and forced to live in homeless shelters. The nexus between government regulators and special interests reaches down to even the local level. I suspect that I would have little difficulty convincing young Nathan about the problems associated with government regulation and its connection to special interests.

Government bureaucracies seem to naturally oppose anything that might make people less dependent on them. The interests of the people always take a back seat to the primacy of government authority. Activities that would have been applauded and held up as examples to be emulated are now suppressed because they trespass on some government agency's turf.

In Philadelphia, the "City of Brotherly Love," Angela Prattis must pay $1,000 to appear before a board hearing and was threatened with fines of $600 per day because she was *giving free lunches to needy children* in her neighborhood without first obtaining permission from the city bureaucrats.

19. Opposition to Reform

To you and to me the idea of reforming this obvious circumvention of our Constitution might seem like a really good idea; but there will be many powerful people to whom it will be a serious threat. Millions of government workers will view this reform much differently from how we see it. Many powerful politicians who benefit greatly from collaborating with the bureaucracy will fight against reform. Even businesses that have close ties to government regulators will fight to maintain the status quo and to retain the advantage they now have over competitors. These people can be ruthless and have access to unlimited funds — often our tax dollars — with which to fight us.

To appreciate how much incentive the bureaucrats actually have to fight us, and how much is at stake for them, consider that of every one of the trillions of dollars that we have "spent" on our welfare programs, seventy-two cents ($.72) went to administrative costs and only twenty-eight cents ($.28) went to the actual targeted welfare recipients. If these bureaucrats actually wanted to help poor people wouldn't that distribution of monies be a lot different? Can you see why the bureaucrats will fight tooth and nail to hang on to the gravy train they are on? If you resent the welfare recipients who are supposedly living off your tax dollars, how much more should you resent the folks who are scraping off nearly three-fourths of those tax dollars for themselves while administering the system?

Opponents will tout the numerous (though usually fictional) benefits of all these regulations. They will appeal to the populace to prevent any reform that would weaken government oversight and control on the premise that somehow government agents are more interested in your health and welfare than your friends, family, and neighbors are and only they can protect you. In truth, though, they will be fighting to hold onto the power and privilege they now personally enjoy. Leonid Brezhnev, former Premier of the Soviet Union, said that a man can have enough liquor that he wants no more (for a while anyhow), enough sex that he is satisfied (temporarily, at least); but of power there is never enough—he will always want more. That Mr. Brezhnev was an expert on the subject of power is inarguable.

Politicians who work to advance reforms will face strong opposition from the entrenched establishment. It will require courage and a sincere commitment to stay the course. I believe that the survival of our liberty requires that we find such courageous men and women and elect them to office with the understanding that we will be solidly behind them throughout the fight.

> *Note: This battle can not be won by even the best conservative politicians alone. It requires the committed support of millions of patriotic American citizens who understand what is at stake and are willing to face the tough battles ahead. The recent fight in Wisconsin in the attempted recall of Governor Scott Walker and a few conservative state legislators is a good preview of what we will be dealing with—on a much larger scale.*

I will tell you from first-hand experience that most politicians and candidates will not have the stomach for this battle. Most of them want a not-too-difficult job with lots of prestige and generous rewards. They do not want to crusade to save their country, that would be too hard and risky. Some will give lip service to the cause while campaigning and then drop the issue once elected because it would make them unpopular among the other members of the "elite club" of privileged high officials.

We must have a strategy that anticipates opposition from many fronts.

20. Strategy to Win

If you have read this far and are still reading, you probably have a fairly good understanding of the problem and of how difficult it will be to correct it. You may even have a passionate desire to be a part of the process to fix it. That is good. However, it will take more than just recognizing the problem and being passionate about it to make a difference. It will take a strategy, which will translate into a plan of action, which will translate into measurable results in time. All this must be propelled by a lot of work, some sacrifice, and possibly even some suffering. I hesitated to mention that last item because it sounds a bit ominous; but the reality is that the opponents of reform will not go down quietly, that is for certain.

Our strategy involves three components:
- Lines of Attack

- Justification

- Reagan's Secret Weapon

I propose that a three-pronged attack is most likely to succeed. One prong is the Legislative route. Congressmen and, to a lesser degree, Senators in the US Legislature can be made aware of the importance of this issue by us. It will take a lot of us to do that; but we can have an influence on them. We individual citizens, regardless what other differences we may have, must band together into organized groups to lobby our elected officials (not just in the US Legislature, either, in State legislatures and other State-level offices) to let them know that we want reform. We must also be specific as to exactly what reforms we want. I realize that lots of us have shouted about lots of issues in the past and we were often ignored; but I assure you that if enough of us are organized for a single purpose (setting aside other difference we might have), we will be heard. Members of the House of Representatives will listen sooner than Senators will; but eventually we can get the ear of even them.

I have already had contact with a number of officeholders and leading candidates for office who do understand this problem and are sympathetic to our cause. They are now a small minority; but working with and through them we will be able to enlist more and more. Because they understand how much resistance we will all face, it is critical that they know that there is a huge, organized body of citizens behind them. It is much easier for them to fight courageously if they know that there is an army behind them.

The US Legislature has the ability to reform Administrative Law. If we succeed via this route, that will be terrific; however, I would not rely solely on this first prong of the attack. For one thing the current President has demonstrated a willingness to completely ignore the Legislature and to use the Bureaucracy to go around them entirely. (For example, refer to the discussion about new CO_2 limits for electric generation.) For another, the US Senate is still under control of non-conservatives and with six-year terms and the overwhelming advantage of incumbency, making a major change to the Senate can take many years.

The second prong is the Judicial route—the Supreme Court. Powers of the central government were granted by the States; thus I believe it must be the States that pursue this line via the Supreme Court. The structural change that the New Deal Administrative Law imposed represents a massive transfer of powers from the States to the Federal Government. As a result, Federal agencies routinely usurp State powers through the regulations they impose. Since Federal powers were granted by the States, it is the States that must challenge to recover their rightful powers in the Supreme Court of the US.

REFORM, NOT REPEAL

I should be clear that our goal is *not* to have the Court repeal the laws that empower federal agencies. I have conceded that some agencies are necessary and that some regulations are desirable. Our goal is to get the Court to order reforms that bring the Fourth Branch into the system of checks and balances intended by our Founders and compliant with the spirit of our Constitution.

In a recent Supreme Court action involving the redistricting of political districts in Texas, the Supreme Court ordered a lower court to modify its decision giving more consideration to the Texas legislature's plan. The Texas legislature had designed political districts, as is its lawful duty. Some people objected to the legislature's district map on the basis that it did not give enough consideration to predominantly minority areas. A legal battle ensued and a three-judge panel in a federal court re-drew the entire map according to the wants of the minorities. The state challenged the court's actions and took the matter to the Supreme Court hoping that the Supreme Court would throw out the lower court's judgment. What the Supreme Court did was to return it to the lower court with instructions to re-do the map giving more deference to the state legislature's desires.

We do not expect, or desire, for the Court to overturn what was done in 1933 and in the decades that followed. We want the Court to demand that the US Legislature modify the laws so as to give deference to the intentions of the Founding Fathers and the Constitution, much as they ordered the lower court in Texas to modify what it had done.

HELP FROM HAMILTON

The Supreme Court's principle duty is to uphold the Constitution by ensuring that all laws passed in the nation are properly consistent with the Constitution and the intentions of the Founders and of the people who ratified it. This is sometimes called "Original Intent." A related principle called "Original Meaning" addresses slightly more detailed issues regarding language usage at the time a text was written; but I will consider that as part and parcel of Original Intent.

Alexander Hamilton engraving on our ten-dollar bills

Much debate in Supreme Court cases involves Original Intent. To resolve these debates the Justices of the Court often refer to documents written after the Constitution was drafted supporting the ratification of the Constitution, called The Federalist Papers. These papers were published in newspapers and read and discussed widely. They were intended to clarify the meaning of the words written in the Constitution and how they should and would be interpreted by future courts. The Federalist Papers were written by Alexander Hamilton, John Jay, and James Madison. The most frequently cited of them by Supreme Court Justices is Federalist #78, titled, "The Judiciary Department," written by Alexander Hamilton. The debates between the authors of the Federalist papers and the opposing views expressed in the Anti-Federalist Papers led to the addition of the Bill of Rights and subsequent ratification of the Constitution.

> The Federalist Papers defended the Constitution and supported ratification of it. Therefore, they define the meaning of what was written in the Constitution as it was understood at the time it was ratified.

Federalist #78 explains that since the powers of the Federal Government are limited, if it creates a law that exceeds its defined powers, that law is void and the judiciary must side with the Constitution and against that law. (Lawyers might use the term *void on its face*.) Essentially, it reassures the States and the public that the Constitution is sufficient to prevent unwanted expansion of the central government. Since this reassurance contributed to the eventual ratification of the Constitution, Hamilton's explanation can be taken to describe the intentions of both the authors of the Constitution and of those people who voted to ratify it.

> As an illustration of the following point, I often ask: if you do not have the right to go into your neighbor's house and take whatever you want, can you give the right to do that to your children or to anyone else? Of course not! You can not give anyone a right that you yourself do not first possess. When government officials do something like that, lawyers use the term *ultra vires*, meaning that they acted beyond their powers or jurisdiction, thus, their action was invalid, *void on its face*. Any action taken as a result or as a byproduct of such a voided action is itself void. Today that describes most of the rules and regulations

issued by the Bureaucracy and most of the enforcement tactics employed based on them.

Remember that in 1933 Administrative Law gave powers to Federal Agencies to make and enforce rules and regulations without regard for whether or not they were within the defined powers of the Federal Government. I ask you now: If an entity does not have the power (authority, jurisdiction) to do something, can it grant that power to an agency that is a part of itself? Would doing so not completely nullify the constitutional limits on its powers?

> *"...courts of justice, whose duty it must be to declare all acts contrary to the manifest tenor of the Constitution void." –* Federalist #78

If Federalist #78 is so frequently cited, does that not say it is highly regarded by the Justices? And, if it is, does that not dictate that the Administrative Laws that function as we described must be "void," and that the Justices *must* side against them or themselves be in violation of the Constitution?

The fact that Hamilton may have underestimated the ingenuity and cunning of future politicians, or overestimated the fealty to the Constitution of life-appointed Justices, does not mitigate the point that his words do define Original Intent since they were obviously accepted as being accurate by those who ratified the Constitution. It is not required that Original Intent be based on perfect reasoning.

Again, we do not want the Court to overturn the laws; but rather to direct the Legislature to make them more consistent with the letter of and spirit of our Constitution, which clearly never intended there to be an organ of government that is exempted from Article I, Section 8, the "Enumerated Powers" section.

The powers granted to the federal government were granted from the States. The powers assumed by the federal government through Administrative Law were appropriated from the States. Since the challenge in the Court must then come from the States, we must enlist allies within State governments by lobbying all State legislators and other state officials telling them that we want our state to join with other states in the suit for reform.

The third prong is our "nuclear option." The Constitution provides that if two-thirds (currently 34) of the legislatures of the States demand it, there must be called a convention for proposing amendments to the Constitution. Then, if three-fourths (currently 38) of the States ratify it, an Amendment becomes part of our Constitution.

Since the overreach of federal regulation adversely affects all fifty states in many ways, there should be a sufficient number of State legislatures that would join the call for reform. It is, after all, principally State powers that are being co-opted by the central government.

Our work to enlist state legislators and other state-level officials to our cause would contribute to this nuclear option if the less grand options did not succeed. In fact, once sufficient support has been garnered, the *threat* of the nuclear option would add weight to our other efforts.

Ronald Reagan's secret weapon always was his ability to connect with the People. Once we have won over enough of the People (translates to "voters" to politicians) to our cause, we will see that opponents are not as eager to oppose the reforms and supporters become much more vocal and energized in their support.

21. Impact of Regulations

To justify making rules and regulations to control our business and private lives, government always presents them as the solution to some problem. Sometimes the problem is a genuine problem and sometimes (very rarely) the regulations are a legitimate solution or, at least, an appropriate step to address the problem. More often, though, the problem is one concocted to justify yet another regulation and expansion of government powers, or it is an inappropriate remedy to a real problem.

At the time of this writing our country is in its third year of a massive recession (which some economists describe as actually being more likely a depression) that started with what is called the "Sub-Prime Lending Collapse." What happened was that mortgage lenders and banks had been making real estate loans to people who were not qualified for those loans. The loans were then bundled by giant financial institutions into what they called investment-grade securities that were labeled "Triple-A" and sold to all sorts of investors, both domestic and foreign, both individual and institutional. Of course, such a scheme had to collapse eventually, and when it did the effects were devastating — not just in the US, but worldwide.

This economic crisis was used by powerful federal officials to justify massive new regulations that greatly increase the control that government has over all financial institutions and virtually merge big government with big finance in an unholy marriage. The statist argument that justified such a move was that Wall Street and the banks hade caused the crisis; thus stronger regulation by government was needed to prevent that ever happening again.

The irony is that the entire crisis was *caused by federal regulations* in the first place. <u>It was not too little regulation; but too much regulation that led to the collapse.</u> Here is a quick synopsis of how that happened.

Back in the time of Jimmy Carter's presidency, in 1977, the federal do-gooders noticed what they deemed to be a problem. Lenders were avoiding making loans in certain geographic areas and communities. It happens that those communities usually had a predominance of minority residents. The practice was called "redlining" because of maps that marked the high-risk areas in red.

For many months we heard news stories on TV deriding this practice as discriminatory against minority citizens until sufficient hype was stirred up for the government to enact a new law, The Community Reinvestment Act (CRA), requiring lenders to encourage business with these "disadvantaged" borrowers. The working assumption was that the banks were motivated to avoid loans to these people and in these areas by racial bigotry; but of course, their real motivation was the much higher risk that the loans would not be repaid and that the collateral would not be adequate to recover the losses. It was borne of experience, not of bigotry.

Notice that in the beginning the law seemed reasonable. It provided that the banks continue to work within prudent business standards and to qualify borrowers appropriately and to maintain safe, sound operation. All of the enforcement of this law was carried out by federal agencies, like The Federal Reserve Bank, Federal Deposit Insurance Corporation, and others. Because the law stipulated that the lenders continue safe and prudent business practices, as they had been doing prior to the law, not much was really changed at first.

Then came a new crisis, the Savings & Loan Crisis, in the 1980's. Government uses every crisis to ratchet up its powers and its control over us. President George H.W. Bush signed the Financial Institutions Reform and Recovery Act of 1989. This greatly advanced the cause of government control over lenders by making their records regarding lending to disadvantaged groups much more available to any group or organization wanting to pressure them to become more "compliant" or to present them as being discriminatory (racially).

Then, under President Clinton in the 1990's, momentum was gathering for more and more government control over lending and a series of acts were passed, each one moving the ball forward a few more yards. Acts involving the FDIC and Resolution Trust Corporation (RTC) made losing money through compliance with the CRA a virtue by giving them credit for money lost on loans and other business in the disadvantaged areas or to women.

Then, in 1992, came the move that practically guaranteed that a massive economic collapse would occur at some time in the not-too-distant future. The Federal Housing Enterprises Financial Safety and Soundness Act required that Fannie Mae and Freddie Mac, quasi-government corporations that made real estate loans, must buy loans made in disadvantaged areas from lenders who made them. This meant that there was a ready market for bad loans. The normal business reasoning that would make lending money to people you knew would not repay it a business error was entirely nullified. Banks could make all the bad loans they were able to make, then immediately sell them to Fannie or Freddie and thus have no risk and remain totally compliant with the nonsensical federal regulations.

Soon thereafter, then Attorney General Janet Reno began attacking lenders with the power of the Justice Department threatening *criminal* action against bank officers if they did not meet quotas of loans, now known as "sub-prime loans," in their areas. The result, of course, was millions of junk loans made by lenders, then bought by Fannie and Freddie, which were being propped up by our tax dollars.

The descriptive term "sub-prime" refers to the qualifications of the borrower. A "prime" loan would be one in which the borrower's income, credit rating, payment history, and other criteria place him/her in the low-risk category for a lender. Sub-prime indicates the opposite—the borrower's profile does *not* qualify him/her as a low-risk borrower—but rather, as a high-risk borrower. The government rules actually required lenders to make loans by ignoring these things, which even led to what was called "no-doc" loans.. No-doc meant "no documentation" for income or other criteria. A borrower could simply state an income on the loan application, truthfully or not, and thus qualify for a loan.

So it was laws and regulations by the federal government that *caused* the economic collapse that was then used to justify more laws and regulations.

In 2010, the Dodd–Frank Wall Street Reform and Consumer Protection Act was passed in response to the economic situation and massive government bailouts that resulted from earlier government regulation of banking and lending.

Interestingly, both the named authors/sponsors of this act, Senator Chris Dodd and Congressman Barney Frank, were heavily involved in the malfeasance that caused the crisis in the first place and now their power was further enhanced as they were made the principle captains of the government interventions purportedly meant to correct the very problems that they created. Dodd-Frank also creates new agencies (such as the Consumer Financial Protection Bureau) that are not subject to any oversight by Congress.

"In history, nothing happens by accident. If it happened, you can bet someone planned it." – *Franklin Delano Roosevelt*

This is entirely consistent with my premise that a government solution to a problem almost never results in a problem solved, it actually guarantees that the problem will persist and will likely be used to rationalize the need for yet more government regulation.

In 2008 President Obama said that when his plans regarding energy were implemented "electric rates will necessarily skyrocket" and promised that he would "bankrupt owners of coal-fired plants." Today, unreasonable regulations regarding the level of CO_2 (a normal component of our atmosphere) emissions from electric generation plants are designed to accomplish precisely that. How and when did it become a legitimate objective of our federal government to bankrupt a very critical industry for our nation and to force the price of electricity that powers our homes and businesses so high as to bankrupt every middle class citizen and small business in our country?

This blatant attack on our economy by crippling our electric-generating capability comes while that same government is using tax dollars to subsidize electric-driven automobiles.

Can we find any way to rationalize these contradictions that does not paint a picture of an out-of-control central government utilizing a bloated and unrestrained bureaucracy to beat its own citizenry into submission? If you can think of one, as Ross Perot once said: "I'm all ears."

Lest you think that government regulations only attack major corporations or industries, let's take a look at what your government has done recently to protect you. Just this year, the Food and Drug Administration (FDA) concluded a yearlong sting operation that culminated in shutting down Rainbow Farms, a Pennsylvania Amish dairy. Were they making explosives? No. Were they plotting the overthrow of our government? No. Then what were they doing wrong? They were selling raw milk to natural food advocates who believe that raw milk is better for your health. Mind you, this attack on an Amish dairy was conducted as if they were attacking an organized crime operation with undercover agents masquerading as health food fanatics buying milk using assumed names, and surveillance, and surprise inspections in the middle of the night.

Actually, this is only one instance of our federal bureaucracy attacking individuals and small businesses that produce food products. If they have their way, the bureaucracy will control every morsel of food that every American eats making every American totally dependent on the government for bare necessities and survival.

The bureaucracy is entirely hostile to the concepts of rugged individualism, or self sufficiency. This is in severe contrast to the stance our government took during World War II, when it encouraged even city-dweller citizens to have a "victory garden" so as to be able to grow at least some of the food they would require to last out the war.

Even disaster preparedness is being outlawed by the federal monster. For farmers who live in northern climates, it is standard operating procedure to have enough non-perishable food, water, medicines, and supplies of every sort always on hand in case of a disaster. Blizzards can shut a family into their home for many days or even weeks at a time. In other parts of the country we have seen tornadoes, hurricanes, and floods cripple entire communities. The threat of terrorist attack offers just one added scenario to the list of possible disasters that one should be prepared to live through. The practice of maintaining survival provisions on hand has become widespread across the nation. Most people call it "preparing," or "prepping" for short. Our government takes a much more hostile view of it and calls it "hoarding" and is actively identifying "hoarders" and classifying them as potential terrorists. Executive Orders (EO's) authorize seizing all stored food (EO 10998) in event of a declared emergency, which includes a financial crisis (EO 11051), which, as we have seen, can be initiated by the government.

Because Preppers are not usually very outspoken about what they are doing, it is not possible to give an accurate count of how many American citizens are taking at least some steps toward being prepared to sustain their families during a disaster; but there is evidence that it is a significant portion of our population, and growing. All these people who are merely concerned for the survival of their loved ones are being viewed as if they were enemies and can expect more and more new regulations designed to attack them and to impede their efforts in the future.

Rather than being prepared to survive an emergency, the government would prefer that you depend on government services, like the Federal Emergency Management Agency (FEMA, now a part of Homeland Security) for your survival. But last summer when wildfires were raging across Texas, FEMA and other federal agencies actually acted to retard efforts to quench the fires. Because Texas is politically targeted by the

Obama Administration, relief workers and equipment from other states were prevented from coming to Texas' aid. Fire-fighting aircraft that were slated to come to drop water on Texas fires were grounded in California by a bogus strike that the federal government had the power to set aside in light of the emergency; but chose not to. Other relief workers and fire fighters from other states were similarly impeded in coming to help Texas, in spite of the fact that Texas routinely runs to the aid of other states when they are struck by disasters.

Should we really feel secure relying on the politically-motivated federal agencies?

Joseph Stalin explained how to control the people

When Joseph Stalin assumed power in Russia, he is reputed to have delivered a speech to his generals. He held, the story goes, a live chicken while he spoke and methodically plucked the feathers from the chicken as he talked and as the audience watched. Then he dropped the chicken to the floor and it soon crowded close to his legs.

He explained that this was how to control the people. If the chicken walked into the sun, it was too hot on its un-feathered skin. If he walked into the shade, it was too cold without feathers to keep it warm. It clung close to his legs to be in shade and close to the warmth of his body. It was totally dependent upon him for survival.

Could it be that Stalin's lesson has found a receptive audience in our modern-day government?

22. Attacking the Source

If you listen to politicians who are sympathetic to the problem of overregulation speak, you will notice that most of them will talk about challenging the regulations or rules themselves. Since the federal agencies have the power to create tens of thousands of new regulations each year, trying to defeat them by fighting one regulation at a time is definitely a losing battle.

Some more ambitious politicians will talk about abolishing this or that agency or department, often without any specifics as to how that can be done. That sounds like a much more satisfying plan; but since the federal government creates new agencies hundreds at a time, this battle plan is also destined to fail.

The only way to actually solve the problem is to *find the source* and attack there. In fact, that is true of most problems. Determining the source is one of the key elements to effective problem solving.

In the case of federal regulation overreach, the regulations are merely the symptom of the problem. Even the agencies themselves are merely a symptom. It is the Administrative Law, which I believe to be constitutionally questionable in its current form, that is the source of the problem. That is what enables the creation of these agencies and it is what empowers them to make what should properly be called "laws" bypassing the protocol our Constitution provided to protect us from a tyrannical government and what the Founders called an "Imperial Presidency."

23. Finding Support

"All that is necessary for the triumph of evil is that good men do nothing." – *Edmund Burke*

Regardless which prong of our attack succeeds, it will have required the support of millions of American citizens to prod government officials to fight toward our goal. The majority of elected and appointed officials are reluctant to pursue any mission that will be long and difficult with political risks attached. We citizens must provide a constant, relentless incentive for them to press on.

There are thousands of groups of politically interested people in our country. Many are focused on a single issue. The problem is that these various activist groups have great difficulty coordinating their efforts with other groups passionate about a different issue. The good thing is that the issue of reforming Administrative Law should appeal to most of them, possibly for different reasons. In fact, it should be able to attract supporters from both major political parties, liberal and conservative, and from across the economic spectrum. The intrusion of rules and regulations from "above" is so pervasive that almost every person in the nation is somehow affected adversely, whether they realize it or not.

The strategy for enlisting supporters should be based upon identifying specific regulations that are abhorrent to each particular interest group and focusing on those points when addressing the corresponding groups of people. Those passionate about energy independence, for instance, might not be aroused to action by a regulation against selling raw milk; but they would respond to regulations limiting carbon dioxide or methane release when drilling for or refining gas and oil. Home Schoolers may not get fired up about those issues; but they would respond to regulations involving education, and so forth. I will point out a few such interest groups and the sort of regulations and rules that might spur them to join the battle to reform Administrative Law.

OIL AND GAS PRODUCERS

Anyone involved in the drilling, refining, transporting, or even using petroleum products will be acutely aware of federal regulations that seem to be designed not to improve Americans' lives, but to hamper domestic energy production. These regulations make it extremely risky to undertake any activity that develops domestic energy and they keep our nation dependent on foreign oil. Unrealistic restrictions on the amount of methane that may be released to the atmosphere in the process of drilling and frac'ing serve no real purpose; but they prevent many producers from operating. Methane is a normal component of our atmosphere and is naturally produced by such ordinary processes as cow belching (or other gaseous emissions from living creatures). the principle component of the gas that we are drilling for is methane. It is inevitable that some tiny amounts of methane will be released into the atmosphere during the process and there is no valid reason to criminalize it.

All of the regulations and rules that are hampering our energy production unnecessarily are issued by agencies empowered by Administrative Law. They include EPA, Department of Energy, Fish and Wildlife, and others. No energy producer wants to damage the environment.

I am convinced that the reform of Administrative Law will lead rapidly to the rescission of countless harmful regulations that hamper energy production and, thus, to full energy independence for our nation within a few years. The US has the largest volume of oil and gas reserves of any nation on Earth. We have the latest technology for recovering it and refining it efficiently and cleanly.

RESERVES OF FOSSIL FUELS PLUS TECHNICALLY RECOVERABLE UNDISCOVERED OIL AND NATURAL GAS

source: Congressional Research Service - document R40872, 2009

Rank	Country	Total Fossil Fuel Proved Reserves	Est. Undiscovered Oil and Gas (Billion BOE)	Total Fossil Fuels (Billion BOE)
1	USA	969.7	351.5	1321.3
2	Russia	954.9	293.7	1248.6
3	China	465.6	28.4	494
4	Saudi Arabia	311.6	231.3	543
5	Iran	311.6	114.3	425.9
6	Canada	214.1	7.2	221.3

Note: since this data was compiled in 2009 additional oil and gas that is technically recoverable has been discovered in the US, which would improve our numbers even further.

Note: BOE means Barrel of Oil Equivalent

ELECTRICITY PRODUCERS & USERS

Anyone involved in the production of electric power is aware of federal regulations limiting the production of carbon dioxide in the generation of electricity. A third to half our electric generation is coal-fired in the US. New regulations stipulate that a plant may not produce more than 1,000 pounds of CO_2 (carbon dioxide) per megawatt of power generated. The typical coal-fired plant produces 18 times that much now. To retrofit plants with after processors to reduce CO_2 emissions would cost billions of dollars per plant. These restrictions in effect shut down a large portion of our electric production using the least-expensive fuel available, coal. Coal-fired electric generating plants produce what is considered the "baseline" electric power for our country because of the low cost. Variances in demand are satisfied by other sources, chiefly gas-fired generation. Nuclear generation accounts for about one-fifth of overall US electricity production; but political and regulatory issues make it nearly impossible to add new nuclear power plants.

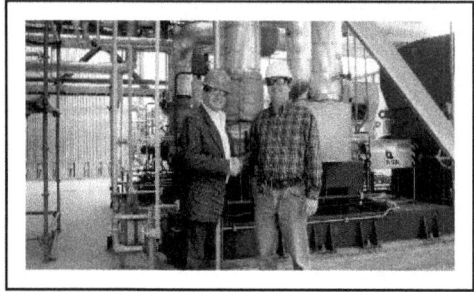

Your author at a state-of-the-art electric power plant using combined-cycle gas-fired generators

It should be mentioned that CO_2 is not a poison. It is the gas that we animals exhale and plants ingest in order to use as a component for photosynthesis, which produces, among other things, oxygen (that we breathe). Arguments that CO_2 is a greenhouse gas that we must limit production of are specious. CO_2 is indeed a greenhouse gas; however it makes up about 2% of all greenhouse gasses. Water vapor is by far the most abundant greenhouse gas and has a far larger impact on our planet's climate. Additionally, all of human production of CO_2 could not increase the amount in the atmosphere more than a tiny fraction of a percent since many natural processes produce it constantly.

All of the nonsensical regulations and restrictions that hamper our electric production and increase our cost of electric power are from agencies empowered by Administrative Law. Electric power is necessary for nearly every aspect or our lives and businesses. Anyone familiar with the electric generation industry has a very real interest in the reform of Administrative Law.

Since coal is generally the most economical fuel used to generate electricity, and since it is under a full frontal attack by federal regulations, it might be interesting to note that the US has the largest reserve of coal in the world. Here are the top five countries having significant coal resources.

TOP FIVE NATIONAL COAL RESERVES

expressed in native units and as billions of barrels of oil equivalent (BOE)

Country	(billion short tons)	as BOE
United States	262.7	906.3
Russia	173.1	597.2
China	126.2	435.4
Australia and New Zealand	85.1	293.6
India	62.3	214.9

source: Congressional Research Service - document R40872, 2009

ADVOCATES FOR ENERGY INDEPENDENCE

The following consumption statistics, viewed in conjunction with the data above for coal, and gas & oil reserves shows that there is no reason to fret over running out of energy resources in the US even if we totally cut off all purchases from other countries. Although we have enough coal, oil, and gas to meet one-hundred percent of our needs for hundreds of years to come, unnecessary regulations based upon junk science or no science at all attacking every aspect of our energy production industries is forcing America to buy energy from nations that do not like us. The money we pay to them is often used against us in many ways: economic, political, and military (including supporting terrorism against the US).

Energy independence is not only important for our economic future, it is critical to national security.

UNITED STATES ANNUAL CONSUMPTION OF OIL, NATURAL GAS, AND COAL

source: Congressional Research Service - document R40872, 2009

Resource	Production	Consumption
Oil	2.46 billion barrels/year (2.46 billion BOE)	7.1 billion barrels/year (7.1 billion BOE)
Natural Gas	20.6 trillion cubic feet/year (3.7 billion BOE)	23.2 trillion cubic feet/year (4.1 billion BOE)
Coal	1.17 billion short tons/year (4.0 billion BOE)	1.04 billion short tons/year (3.6 billon BOE)

Values are for year-end, 2008

You can see from a comparison of this chart to the one showing our reserves that even without any improvements in the technology for recovering oil and gas, for instance, we have enough for well over 100 years at our current rate of consumption. Potential improvements in our technology for recovering fossil fuels and for the efficiency of using them could, and probably will, extend that much longer. Of course, recent new discoveries of vast reserves within the US also greatly expand our timeline as well.

You may notice that the size of our reserves is expressed in Barrels of Oil Equivalent. That is because in many applications oil, gas, and coal can be interchangeable. For instance, you can use any of them to generate electricity. Many generating plants actually do use a combination of coal and gas to improve efficiency and reduce emissions.

Natural gas can be used very efficiently and cleanly to generate electricity, especially in a modern combined-cycle generating plant. But unnecessary regulations against accidentally releasing methane into the atmosphere threaten to shut down gas drilling and recovery operations. The US has the largest reserve of natural gas of any nation on Earth.

Natural gas can be used, and is used in millions of automobiles worldwide, as a super-clean and efficient substitute for gasoline or diesel fuel. Federal regulations make it unnecessarily cumbersome and expensive to power US vehicles using natural gas even though many other countries are using it very successfully.

Interestingly, the conversion of a standard gasoline engine to run on natural gas is rather simple. Also, because natural gas as a fuel for an automobile engine has a higher octane rating (about 120-130 octane) than ordinary gasoline, it is possible to get even more power from an automobile engine by also increasing its compression ratio. Most conversions do not bother with that step as it is more costly to do than a simple conversion of the fuel injection; but if natural gas were to become commonly available to drivers, we could expect to see automobiles manufactured with engines designed to take advantage of the higher octane rating. America's vast reserve of natural gas, which is much easier and cheaper to refine than oil, could power our automobiles for hundreds of years — cleanly and at lower cost. All the technology exists and is proven. Unnecessary Federal regulations are the only real obstacle.

> Note: I just wanted to add a word about my attitude toward energy independence. I believe that the US could and should develop the capacity to produce all of the energy that we need to function at full speed; but that does not mean that we should abolish all commerce regarding energy with friendly countries. Trade with our friends is good for us in many ways, including giving us some reliable sources to turn to in the event that weather or other types of disasters should put some of our own production or refining capability out of service temporarily. Of course, it also strengthens our relationships with those other countries.

PROPERTY OWNERS

Ownership of private property was cited by John Locke as fundamental for liberty. Locke was an inspiration for many of our Founding Fathers, all of whom shared this belief regarding property rights. Without ownership of private property citizens can not provide for their most basic needs of food, shelter, and defense, and are dependent upon their overseers for life itself. Such a dependency is antithetical to any notion of personal freedom

Ownership of property must include control over its use. Thus, if you own a plot of land you must have the ability to use it as you see fit for your own purposes, within reason of course.

Regulations that claim to be intended to preserve our environment are being used to prevent property owners from even the most sensible utilization of their own property. Mud puddles are classified as protected wetlands. Common reptiles and vermin become endangered species. Ordinary trees are determined to be the only acceptable habitat for a bird that actually makes a happy home nearly anywhere it lands.

Additionally, the federal government now owns about 29% of all US real estate — over 650 million acres. Most of the oil and gas producing land is included in this. While there may be a valid reason for the federal government to own *some* land, it is probably true that a much smaller share of all US land would suffice.

SMALL BUSINESS OWNERS

Many federal regulations actually work to crowd out small (and medium-sized) businesses in favor of a few large, favored corporations. Small business is actually the most important category of businesses in our country. Eighty percent (80%) of jobs are created in small businesses and most of the innovation that leads to improvements in our lives comes out of small enterprises struggling to make a place for themselves.

Because the corporate giants have the money and political connections to influence what federal agencies do, and because many of the heads of these agencies are drawn from those corporate giants, the actions of these agencies more often benefits the big guys at the expense of the little guys.

For example, the recent Dodd-Frank Financial Reform includes a regulation on bank debit card fees. The regulation limited fees to $.24 per transaction on the premise that that was the actual cost to the banks. In fact, the per-transaction costs are lower for the giant banks than they are for small local banks and the giant banks have numerous other fee structures to compensate for the reduced revenue from debit card fees. Thus, this new regulation gave the banking giants another advantage over their smaller competitors. We can be certain that it was crafted with plenty of input from lobbyists from the mega-banks.

Owners and employees of small- and medium-sized companies have a large interest in the reform of Administrative Law.

GASOLINE USERS

Gasoline and diesel prices in our country have doubled in the past few years, largely because we are dependent on oil from other countries, most of which are unfriendly to us. As mentioned earlier, there is no reason why the US should not be energy independent. We have far more oil reserves than any other country and all the technology to recover and refine it efficiently. Federal regulations that purport to protect the environment or some lizard or bug are preventing exploration and production of oil in America.

The US Department of Interior (DOI) continues to impose mindless restrictions on offshore drilling for oil, thus crippling American energy production and forcing us to buy expensive oil from countries that are not hampered by such restrictions and could even be drilling in the same waters that US companies are prevented from drilling in. The moratorium is based on junk science that even federal courts have dismissed; but DOI continues renewing it because the Bureaucracy does not even need to offer a reason for what it does any longer, it just does whatever it wants to do.

Reform of Administrative Law would result in increased American oil production and decreased prices for gasoline. People in businesses that use gasoline, diesel, or fuel oil (such as truckers and heavy equipment operators) have a huge interest in the reform of Administrative Law.

REAL ESTATE OWNERS

One of the fundamental principles underlying our liberty is the right to own property. Owning property means that you have control over it and may use it as you see fit. You may build upon it, farm it, hunt on it, or dam a creek to make a pond, if you wish. Of course, we can not deny that there is a proper place for some restrictions. If you owned a lot in a downtown area and wanted to raise pigs on it, you might be seriously disturbing your neighbors.

But it is best if the restrictions on your land use be decided and administered locally by city, county, or state government, rather than by the federal government. There are numerous instances of individuals being prosecuted for doing what most reasonable people would consider normal and lawful things regarding a piece of land they own. Filling in a low area that floods annually so as to stop mosquito breeding might seem like a good thing to do; but when the federal bureaucracy decides that that muddy swamp is a "protected wetland," doing a very reasonable thing becomes a crime.

If you are prevented from erecting a building on your land because of the daunting requirements for an Environmental Impact Statement while a large corporation is able to proceed with a similar project on the adjacent land because it has the resources to navigate through the bureaucracy, your ability to use your land as you wish has been unfairly restricted.

The Environmental Impact Statement is an example of how government regulations can present a hurdle that smaller businesses are unable to jump while giant companies can, giving big business a decided advantage over smaller competitors. We can see why influential giant companies might actually have no objection to such regulations and might actually work to help impose them.

After World War II, General Dwight Eisenhower, later to become President Eisenhower, warned us of the dangers presented by the "military-industrial complex." While he was focusing mainly on the giant companies that made billions of dollars selling to the military, we must expand his warning to include companies in *any* industry that are large enough to manipulate government to their advantage.

GUN OWNERS

The Bureau of Alcohol, Tobacco, and Firearms (and Explosives) has imposed a number of restrictions on gun ownership and is attempting to regulate reloading, storing ammunition, attachments to firearms, and sales of firearms. In fact, they have even made moves that are intended to control the very manufacture of firearms and ammunition.

The Second Amendment to the US Constitution guarantees our right to bear arms. Many firearms owners will argue that we have that right so that we can hunt game, shoot for sport, or defend against criminals. All these are certainly true; but the primary purpose for the Second Amendment is not any of those reasons. We have the right to bear arms so that we can defend against tyranny—tyranny from a government that has mutated from one that is for, by, and of the people into one that oppresses its own citizens, as most governments throughout history have done.

Millions of Americans are members of the National Rifle Association and of similar state gun owner organizations. These people are quite aware of the threat that federal regulation poses. For the most part, though, they see the problem in terms of there being too many bad politicians. While there certainly are, the real problem is the empowerment of federal agencies to make and enforce the rules and regulations that are so despised by gun owners.

In fact, we will find that for just about every group of people we address who object to one or another sort of regulation, they attribute the problem incorrectly. Once we educate people as to the actual source of the problem, we will win them to support our mission.

PREPPERS

In recent years a movement has taken hold in America and, although it is unheard of by many, it has grown to immense proportions with millions of supporters and participants. It is an outgrowth of what used to be called "survivalists"; but now encompasses a much wider range of issues and attracts a much larger group of citizens. Some "Preppers," as they are called, spend many thousands, even millions, of dollars preparing themselves and their families for calamity. While most will say they are preparing for natural disasters, in fact virtually all of them are also deeply concerned about the prospects for economic and political collapse and the ensuing breakdown of order. A majority of these ultra-realists would point to harmful government actions as a likely primary or contributing cause for such a development. Many are also alarmed by recent federal rules and regulations that virtually criminalize such activities as raising your own food, storing ("hoarding") food and medicine, or even questioning the wisdom of relying on our government for safety and security. These are seen (probably correctly) as moves to ensure dependency on government and to stifle efforts at self sufficiency and preparedness.

All these obnoxious rules, and many thousands more, are issued by agencies of the federal government that are empowered by Administrative Law.

While I would never advocate not being prepared, I will suggest that in addition to "prepping," we should all work to prevent the scenario that we dread. Civil breakdown is NOT a pleasant thought, regardless how well prepared we are. An ounce of prevention is worth a pound of cure, as they say. So, while continuing their activities to be prepared for the worst, wouldn't it be a good idea if they also worked to reform the mutated system that is pushing us toward that breakdown.

An interesting statistic to note is that if you tally all the American deaths in all wars starting with and including the Revolutionary War and up to the current date, you will find that about 1.3 million Americans have died in wars. Nearly half of them, over 600,000, died in the Civil War. Civil breakdown is a horror to be avoided *if at all possible*, regardless how prepared you may be.

Preppers are naturally sensitive to the overreach of our government and to its very harmful effects and should be very interested in the reform of Administrative Law.

Not only are government regulations pushing us closer to the apocalypse they dread; but they are also criminalizing their efforts to be prepared to survive it.

HOME- AND PRIVATE-SCHOOLERS

There are plans in motion to require that all children attend government-run public schools. Statists have always opposed any form of school choice, such as vouchers, because they believe that the government should have the power to control education of all children. Some now are talking about requiring that all children attend public, not private schools.

Parents who send their children to private schools and parents who home school their children are doing so in order to give them a better education devoid of the indoctrination that public schools force feed children.

The Department of Education was supposedly established to improve the quality of education in our country. Instead, it has reduced it to the level of some third-world countries. The regulation of our schools by this federal agency was never really intended to improve education — it was intended to turn our schools into training facilities for future generations of citizens who are unable to function without the hand of government to control them.

Parents of children attending public schools who would prefer to have a choice as to which school their child goes to should join with home schoolers and private school parents to fight for reform of the Administrative Law that empowers the very damaging Department of Education.

THOSE WHO CHERISH AMERICAN SOVEREIGNTY

Many of the regulations that are crippling our most fundamental industries are, probably intentionally, bringing the US down toward parity with less-prosperous nations around the world. In fact, the United Nations has for decades been promoting an actual project that seeks to even out the wealth and power on the assumption that the United States unfairly owns and uses more than its fair share of resources, especially energy. The program is called "Agenda 21" and its influence has spread into every level of government in America.

The chief tool used to redistribute wealth and prosperity from us to the rest of the world is government regulations. You can hear the voice of this anti-America policy from the mouth of our own President when he proclaims that America uses 25% of the worlds oil though we only nave 2% of the world's oil reserves. This, of course, is false. From the data we presented earlier, you can see that we have more oil than any other country on Earth. The 2% figure was originally promoted by The Sierra Club and it was wrong then; but since it serves a useful purpose to The Left, they continue to repeat it. In fact, that figure probably represents the percent of the world's "proven" oil reserves at some time in the past. Proven reserves are those that are actually drilled and producing oil at that time.

Since most of the land under which American oil has been found is owned by the federal government and because the federal government has curtailed drilling on that land, the government itself has the power to manipulate the American proven oil reserves figure. A much more meaningful figure would be for American *potential* oil reserves, which means oil that we have found and that we possess the technology to recover, though we may not yet have drilled for it. That figure would yield a many-times higher percentage since we have larger amounts of such reserves than any other country on Earth.

Technology, which is constantly advancing, plays a huge role in the size of our potential oil (and gas) reserves. When oil was first discovered and drilled it was using a method we now call "conventional" drilling. That meant that we drilled down to a pool of oil or gas and pumped it out. When the pool was exhausted, the well was considered to be "dry" and it was capped off. That was that! Geologists knew that there was much more oil down there; but it was trapped in the pores of hard rock and could not be extracted — until American oil men developed a technique to fracture the rock and thus release the encapsulated oil and gas.

The technology for "frac'ing" has been improved greatly. The earliest methods involved explosives; but we now use pressurized fluid (usually water) to fracture the rock. Scientists and engineers are constantly working to improve the methodology and to try other fluids, such as pressurized carbon dioxide (CO_2). The interesting thing is that the CO_2 that environmentalists and government regulators are so concerned about releasing into the atmosphere from the production of electricity can be captured and pumped miles below the surface of the Earth to extract oil from rocks. But, fitting coal-fired electric plants with the equipment to capture that CO_2 is extremely expensive at this time.

Another technological advance that, combined with "hydraulic frac'ing" has vastly increased the amount of oil that we can recover from below our soil is "horizontal drilling." Since the rock in which the oil or gas is trapped is sedimentary, it tends to be in zones that are horizontal. For instance, a zone might be only a few hundred feet in height; but many miles wide, shaped like a giant underground pancake. To tap the oil from that zone using only vertical drilling would require many, many holes and huge expense. An American oil man in the 1940's developed a technique for drilling horizontally. That meant that he could drill vertically to the level at which the mineral was found, and then cause the path of the drill to gradually turn until it was proceeding horizontally through the rock according to a controlled path. Most oil is found at a depth of one to two miles (5,000 - 10,000 feet) or so and the turn required about a quarter of a mile, so to accurately guide the drill bit and shaft at those distances was quite an engineering feat; but American ingenuity came through for us and nearly all oil wells today employ horizontal drilling and hydraulic frac'ing. With the shaft proceeding horizontally through miles of oil impregnated rock, the drillers fracture the rock at many points along its path, thus extracting many times more oil from a single well than was possible before. A very interesting explanation can be found at horizontalshaledrilling.com, if you wish to learn more.

There is also another new technology developing to extract oil from rock using high heat applied in the ground where the oil is trapped in rock. As this technology advances it will further increase America's energy resource.

I tell you all of this not so that you might go into the oil business; but so that you will appreciate the fact that as our technology improves, the size of American potential oil reserves increases greatly. The figures we presented earlier could be revised upward tremendously by even a small improvement in our technology. Our free enterprise capitalist system provides the incentives that lead to just such technological advances.

The rest of the world does not have a shortage of resources, they have a shortage of freedom.

There is absolutely no reason why we should not be entirely energy independent; and no reason why we should feel guilt about the bounty resulting from our own ingenuity, our hard work, and our free enterprise system.

Note: There is far more to be said about Agenda 21; but that is not the topic of this book and I do not want to stray too far afield, so I will leave that for another day.

THOSE WHO CHERISH STATE SOVEREIGNTY

Prior to the New Deal era, the federal government engaged in very little regulation of private business or private lives. Where regulations were appropriate, it was the province of the States to deal with it. The New Deal radically changed that. As we discussed at the beginning of this book, the erosion of States powers and expansion of Federal Powers did not occur entirely over night. One very important shift of powers that helped enable the massive power grab of the New Deal was the passage of the Seventeenth Amendment twenty years prior. That effectively silenced the voices of the States in the Federal Legislature leaving them no good way to resist further usurpations of their powers.

The Founders clearly intended that the States remain sovereign and that they be subordinated to the Federal power only to the extent that was necessary to maintain an orderly association among themselves and a mechanism for collaboration on issues of common interest, such as national defense. All powers granted to the Federal government were granted by the States and they were strictly limited. All powers not specifically so granted were reserved for the States or for the People.

The division of powers between the States and the Federal government accommodated two very important principles:

- the closer to the People the government was, the better the government
- variances between the individual states offered choices to people

The first principle does not presume that state officials are inherently better people than federal officials are. It simply relies on the fact that it will be easier for the People to monitor the behavior of and to replace, when necessary, those who govern them. The further above the People any officeholder is, the more difficult it is to keep track of what they are doing and the less responsive they will be to the wants and needs of the people they govern.

The second principle could really be viewed as anti-monopolistic. Anti-monopolistic in the sense that it opposes government monopoly and encourages competing State governments. In the Colonies that formed the original United States, there was not uniformity among their laws or their religions. In New England the colonists were mainly Puritans who were very strict in their observance of their religion. In the southern colonies people were usually Anglican or Baptist. The colonies between them were predominantly Quaker, Lutheran, or even Jewish. Many of the original laws of these Colonies were heavily influenced by the predominant religious denomination and might even require membership in a specific church as a prerequisite to holding office. If you were, say, a Baptist, and wanted to live in the New World, you would probably prefer to live in Georgia than in Massachusetts. There is a definite benefit to accommodating differences among the States rather than trying to establish one monolithic society in which people have no choices.

The Founders certainly intended to allow the States to govern as they each saw fit and to allow people to migrate to whichever they found most accommodating to their beliefs and attitudes.

CONSTITUTIONALISTS

There is a growing segment or our population that is aware of the erosion of our Constitution and is concerned about it. Most Constitutionalists are, as yet, not aware of how it has happened; but I hope that this book will enlighten them and help them to focus their attention to the actual source of the matter.

Constitutionalists are not just focused on a single issue. They are properly concerned about the general loss of liberty and the tendency of our government to seemingly ignore the limits our Constitution placed on it. I would categorize myself into this group. While I am interested in every one of the issues that I listed here, my real concern is for the much broader problem.

To be focused on only one or two aspects of the entire problem can lead us to attack the symptoms instead of the cause of the problems.

I believe that regulators impose some grossly offensive regulations that they know full well will be struck down by us as a diversionary tactic. While we are distracted by their "red herring," a plethora of other regulations are put in place with little notice.

YOU—AND OTHERS

The above list is only a partial list of groups of people who should become informed about and should rally behind this movement. Virtually every American who cherishes liberty has a stake in this fight. It is hard to think of an area of our lives that is not affected negatively by inexplicable government regulations.

If you doubt that your liberty is actually at stake, please note that an article recently published by Accuracy in Media reported:

> *A study, "Profiles of Perpetrators of Terrorism," commissioned by the Department of Homeland Security identified the following characteristics of potential "terrorists."*

- *Americans who believe their "way of life" is under attack*

- *Americans who are "fiercely nationalistic (as opposed to universal and international in orientation)"*

- *People who consider themselves "anti-global" (presumably those who are wary of the loss of American sovereignty, opposed to the United Nations, etc.)*

- *Americans who are "suspicious of centralized federal authority"*

- *Americans who are "reverent of individual liberty"*

- *People who "believe in conspiracy theories that involve grave threat to national sovereignty and/or personal liberty."*

Does that sound like *your* description of terrorists? The Department of Homeland Security was established supposedly to protect us from terrorists. Now it is being perverted to protect our government *from us*.

If you have read this book to this point, you almost certainly fit one or more of the above descriptions. Actually, you are in good company. Every one of the Founding Fathers would be standing beside you.

> *"The two enemies of the people are criminals and government. So let us tie the second down with the chains of the Constitution so that the second will not become the legal version of the first."* – Thomas Jefferson

Every American who migrated to this country to escape tyranny in Germany, Cuba, Russia, China, Vietnam, Nicaragua, or any other country would be with you, also. They have seen what it means to lose their freedoms. They recognize what is happening to us and they know that America has always been the last refuge of the oppressed. When it is lost, there is no place else to go.

Every American who understands how much our predecessors have sacrificed so that we could live in a free country and also understands that we have an obligation to preserve that freedom for our children and grandchildren should be at your side, as well. For decades we have irresponsibly squandered our liberty on short-term comforts and conveniences and allowed government to take over more and more of our lives. We now realize that we will be leaving our children a world devoid of the luxury of freedom that we enjoyed. The fight to reverse our slide into the abyss of tyranny will not be easy; but we have a moral obligation to both our forefathers and to our children to pass on a country as free and beautiful as was given us.

I hope that the examples I have given in this book at least make the point that the Bureaucracy is actually even more powerful and dangerous to our freedom than the elected officials we tend to focus so much attention on. It regularly just ignores the laws that our elected officials pass, or vote to not pass, and decides its own rules with impunity.

"Extremism in defense of liberty is no vice. Tolerance in the face of tyranny is no virtue." – Barry Goldwater

There is not much time left to stop the ravaging of our freedom that was set in motion in 1933.

24. What You Can Do

"One of the penalties of not participating in politics is that you will be governed by your inferiors." *–Plato*

Being aware of the existence of this Fourth Branch of our government is an important first step. Most Americans are aware that somehow our government is intruding into far too much of our lives; but not aware of how it is managing to do that. If we were fortunate enough to have received a decent education, we know that the Constitution is supposed to protect our liberty; but we may have forgotten that *we are obligated to protect the Constitution.* If we do not remain constantly vigilant and active in protecting what our Founders established for us, we will certainly lose it. This book is a starting point.

Share this book with others. If they can't afford to buy it, loan them yours. I will forgive you. Help us to spread this information far and wide. We are going to need millions of allies across the nation if we are going to win the reforms that are necessary to contain government expansion.

The Signers of the Declaration of Independence pledged their lives, their fortunes, and their sacred honor for the cause of liberty — a liberty that you and I have enjoyed all our lives. Of the 56 men who signed the Declaration of Independence, William J. Federer reports:

What happened to their "lives" and "fortunes"

- *17 lost their fortunes*

- *12 had their homes looted, ransacked and burned*

- *5 were captured by the British as traitors, and tortured before they died*

- *2 lost sons serving in the Continental Army*

- *1 had two sons captured, imprisoned and starved in the hull of a British ship*

- *9 fought and died from wounds or hardships of the Revolutionary War.*

I am hoping that we will be able to save that liberty for a lesser price than they had to pay. To do that, we must act <u>now</u> before it is too late.

Talk to friends and post to FaceBook and other social media sites. Make people aware of the problem and the movement to solve it. If you are a member of a group or organization, raise the subject to the other members on the group's blog or website. Many websites for preppers, hunters, home schoolers, and other common interest groups have thousands, or tens of thousands, of subscribers. Of course, there are politically-centered and industry-centered websites that you might sometimes visit also. On many of them you can post a blog entry or even just a comment to an existing blog posting that a lot of other people will read. This is all free and takes just a few minutes of your time. It is a great way to spread information and contact potential new allies.

Go to our website, ReformAdminLaw.org and subscribe. We will be working toward reform and will be enlisting alliances with sympathetic politicians and officials at the federal, state, and local levels. We need many, many citizens to add their voices and maybe a little volunteer work along the way. We must be organized in order to win. Establishing a central communication medium, such as this site, is necessary to bind us together so we can coordinate our efforts. I will try to make the website a central point of information and news about our efforts and a distribution point for calls to action for projects that might arise.

I also intend to use the website to solicit information from you and other subscribers so that we can stay aware of harmful regulations that are needlessly hurting our businesses and industries and of local efforts at fighting them. Remember, the people fighting against one or two regulations are prime suspects to join with us once they understand that we must fight against *the source* of those regulations in order to win. Remember my analogy in the beginning of this book to the Greek Hydra and also the statistics about how many regulations are added every day. The Hydra could only grow two new heads when you cut one head off. The Bureaucracy can easily add two-hundred regulations in the time it takes you to kill one.

Finally, when the time comes, join our advocacy group that will grow from the body of subscribers of the website once there are sufficient numbers. An advocacy group will be able to apply political pressure on legislators and to help candidates who are sympathetic to our cause in their political campaigns. We will also be able to reinforce officeholders who are working to advance our cause. We will need people to volunteer for many different tasks. We will need to establish an organization hierarchy with chapters for each state. Maybe even for each major city also, so that we are poised to focus on local, state, and federal candidates and officials.

We need people like you who possess three personal attributes. You must be:

- **Persuaded** – that we *can* win

- **Passionate** – that we *must* win

- **Perseverant** – that you will endure until we *do* win

Note: I have already presented our mission to several key conservative political figures and have received a positive response and assurances that they will support us. Please do not think that our cause is hopeless, it is not! Yes, the fight will be difficult and long; but we can and will win with your help.

---

25. The Greatest Enemy

"None are more hopelessly enslaved than those who falsely believe they are free." – Johann Goethe

I have said that we will have numerous and very powerful opponents who will fight ruthlessly to prevent reform. But *they* are not the most formidable enemy we will face.

I was born soon after the close of World War II. It was a different America from what we live in today. We have made such great advances in our technology; but suffered such dismal decline in our character.

When I was young the hunger for self sufficiency and independence, even from our parents, was common. It was *American* to want to be independent! In high school we could not wait to graduate and move out on our own, whether to college or to an apartment of our own. Today, it is common for children to remain attached and dependent on their parents until their 20's, 30's, and sometimes even 40's or longer.

Even as children we were proud of our ability to take care of ourselves. It was normal for our parents to give us chores or duties so that we would know how to do the basic tasks required for survival. I could cook, sew a button on, wash the dishes, and do many other necessary duties in order to be independent when I was very young. I was even proud of the fact. It came in handy when I entered the military, also.

Writing in a letter to John Adams about the circumstances that prevailed in the declining days of the Roman republic, Thomas Jefferson said:

"No government can continue good but under the control of the people; and their people were so demoralized and depraved as to be incapable of exercising a wholesome control." – Thomas Jefferson

Today, children are raised in an environment in which they never have to do or learn any of those things necessary to take care of themselves. Everything is done for them. They are unintentionally trained by their parents to expect their needs to be magically met. They believe they are entitled to be taken care of. Clothes get washed, food is prepared, homes get cleaned, all without any effort or even any thought by most children. Back around the 1970's or 80's it became a source of *pride* for young women to *not* be able to cook. It was shameful to have such a domestic skill. Young men were often even less capable of functioning without the continuing service of their mothers.

Now when parents send their kids off to college they can often expect that their kids will be bringing their dirty laundry "home" to be washed because they do not even know how to run a washing machine or use a laundromat. They probably will have to rely on restaurants for food because they do not know how to shop or cook their own meals. Of course, their parents will be paying for those restaurants.

When the child finishes college, it is not unlikely that he will just move "back home." There is no stigma attached to lacking basic life skills any longer.

As recently as the 1980's, when Reagan was President, the portion of the American population that did not pay any income taxes was just nineteen percent (19%). Today it is forty-seven percent (47%)—nearly half, and rising! That means that almost half our population is living off the generosity of the other half. Many years ago I recall being taught that when we reach the point at which half our population is supporting the other half collapse of our economy will be imminent. The paying half will decide that it is easier to be on the receiving side and their numbers will rapidly drop until the remaining tax-paying minority simply quits altogether. It is frightening to think how close we are to that point.

The concept of dependency has become acceptable. Self sufficiency is *not* the goal of every American any longer. Millions among us are conditioned to be content to rely on the generosity of others or on the government dole. There are families that are into their third and fourth generation of dependency on the government today. It is a way of life. A huge portion of our population feels that they are entitled to a comfortable life without having the responsibility to earn it or fight for it. The words "the world doesn't owe you a living" were once common wisdom. Today they would get you a puzzled, and possibly also resentful, look from many Americans.

> Investor's Business Daily reports that the Senate Budget Committee shows that 107 million Americans (35% of the total population) are now receiving some form of government welfare, not including Medicare or Social Security. That is an increase of 10 million in the past two years.

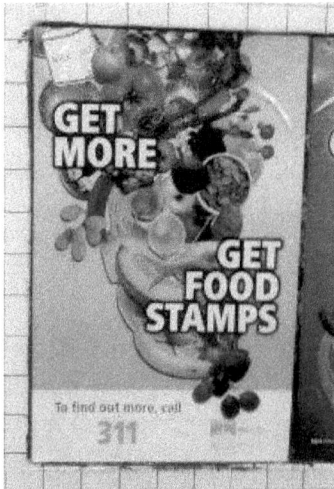

Our government encourages people to become dependent— just dial 311 for Food Stamps!

When you use any online search engine and start typing what you want to look for, it normally tries to anticipate what you will want and presents the most frequently asked questions so that you might be able to select one instead of having to type it all out. If you go into your favorite search engine (Google, AltaVista, Ask, etc.) and start typing: "how do I qualify" you will see that it probably lists the most frequently requested searches. You might be shocked to notice that "food stamps," "welfare," "medicaid," and "disability" will normally be at the top of the list (not necessarily in that order). When I have tried this, the words "college" or "a job" have never yet appeared. This gives you an insight into how many people are scrambling to attach themselves to the government teat and make themselves dependent upon the state.

The greatest enemy we must face will be apathy from Americans who do not mind giving up more and more of their freedom in exchange for momentary comfort, absence of responsibility, and a false security.

"They that can give up essential liberty to obtain a little temporary safety deserve neither liberty nor safety." — Benjamin Franklin

I maintain that there are three ways to enslave people:

- Military Conquest—is expensive and risky and the conquered people will constantly seek ways to break free.

- Indebtedness—involves an outlay of resources and the enslaved will seek ways to gain their freedom.

- Dependency—permanently enslaves people and eliminates the will to break free for all but the most exceptional and rare individuals.

Further, if you can use other people's own money to establish the dependency, the cost to you is nothing. That is exactly what our ever-expanding government is doing to us. Money taken from us as taxes is used for programs that make us rely on government for more and more of our basic needs.

There are so many of our citizens already captured by dependency on government, and satisfied to be so, that it will be very difficult or impossible to win many of them to our cause to restore their freedom.

If you have difficulty imagining how people can so easily be conditioned to accept dependency, think of the residents of New Orleans who, when faced with potentially deadly floods, waited for their government to come and get them rather than take the initiative to evacuate to higher ground themselves. Their dependency is more addictive than a drug, and sometime more deadly.

Fortunately, we *can* win without the support of those terminally dependent people if we succeed in enlisting the support of enough of the others—the freedom-loving citizens of America.

"It does not take a majority to prevail... but rather an irate, tireless minority, keen on setting brushfires of freedom in the minds of men." – Samuel Adams

Those complacent ones do not understand that the comfort and security they enjoy today is like the comfort and security of cattle in a beef herd. One day it will suddenly come to an end and they will find that they exist only for the benefit of their rulers.

As we try to enlist more and more citizens to our cause, we must be prepared to encounter members of this apathetic segment of our population and must realize that we will not be able to win everyone over.

We have all heard stories about very special and rare individuals who broke the shackles of dependency on government largesse and educated themselves and became self-sufficient. Those stories are inspiring; but those people are very rare indeed, maybe one-in-a-million. The vast majority will not have that kind of motivation, courage, and character. We must not allow that to discourage us. One passionate, active supporter is worth more than a gaggle of casual observers.

APATHY THRESHOLD

A second variant of apathy is found in people who *do* recognize the problem and know that we must fix it; but feel that it hasn't yet gotten quite bad enough for them to actually act.

"...all experience hath shown that mankind are more disposed to suffer, while evils are sufferable, than to right themselves by abolishing the forms to which they are accustomed." – Declaration of Independence

They convince themselves that things have not yet reached their threshold of intolerability. They want to hold onto a blissful willing ignorance a little longer. What they are choosing to ignore is that the further down the path toward tyranny we go, the more painful and costly will be the struggle to be free. In fact, there is a point, not far ahead of us now, from which it will be impossible to turn back.

When I talk with people who seem to have this position, I try to point out that by not acting now they are committing their children and grandchildren to fight battles that they themselves selfishly chose to sidestep. To allow others to fight your battles is cowardly and dishonorable—dishonorable to the extreme if those others are your own children.

OMNIPOTENT WEAPONS

> *"Persistence and determination alone are omnipotent. The slogan 'press on' has solved and always will solve the problems of the human race." — Calvin Coolidge*

Press on past those folks that you can not win over to our cause and you will eventually connect with some who possess the same passion for liberty as we have. I assure you that they *are* out there.

> *"Honor, justice, and humanity, forbid us tamely to surrender that freedom which we received from our gallant ancestors, and which our innocent posterity have a right to receive from us." — Thomas Jefferson*

26. A Living Book

While I definitely do not agree with Woodrow Wilson's view that the Constitution should be a "living document" that is subject to re-interpretation based on the political climate of the day, I do think that *this book* should be a living document. You, the reader, will find mistakes and omissions—I have no doubt. You will think of many things that ought to have been included. Therefore, I am publishing this book using methods that allow for updates and revisions to be made easily.

It will be offered using a "print on demand" system that produces your book from the most current manuscript at the time you order it. It will also be offered in *e*Book formats that can be downloaded to your book reader instantly, always from the most current manuscript.

If you find errors or have suggestions for additions or improvements, please contact me from the website ReformAdminLaw.org and I will periodically update the book and always offer the most current version. In fact, I am soliciting your input!

ATTRIBUTION

In the back of this book I am including a list of references. Most are online. A few involve reading another book or printed document. This is not an exhaustive list of references on the subject; but it should be a very good start for anyone interested in doing his own research.

Every reference I give contains a wealth of valuable information and each will likely spark your imagination and lead you to many other sources of information you could explore. It is not possible for anyone to research every fact involving the topic of Administrative Law and the Fourth Branch of government that it has created. The Federal Register alone is already more than 73,000 pages. Every regulation in it could be the subject of further study into its history, its justification, and its effects on our society and our economy and its constitutional implications.

Some readers of this book might feel compelled to study an aspect of the subject that I did not include or that I did not even think of. I will welcome your input and feedback and, if it leads to an inclusion in a future version of this book, I will try to give credit to any reader who has submitted a contribution that I felt was useful.

Every version of this book is to be considered a prototype for the next version.

Please be aware that even if you submit something that is truly valid and valuable, it might not appear in the next version of the book for a variety of reasons. I might be holding it waiting for more information in order to give a more complete treatment of the subject. I might think it is redundant to something already in the book or something submitted by others. I might even think that it is not germane to the topic at all. Although I agree that I am not infallible; you must understand that I will do my best to give fair consideration to anything that is submitted, and that, in the end, my judgment will prevail.

Please do not be offended if you submit something that I seem to have ignored. I might just believe it is so important as to warrant a book of its own, in which case I will give you credit for your submission in the new book.

Thank you for reading this book. I hope it has motivated you to become involved in this very important cause. I look forward to working with you.

27. Epilogue - Not This Time

Quang Nguyen is a naturalized American citizen. Like many who came here to escape tyranny in their former countries, Quang has an appreciation and a love for what most native-born Americans take for granted and assume can never be lost to them.

Had it not been for the kindness and bravery of American soldiers, Quang would have been, as a young boy, one of the many casualties of vicious oppression of their own citizens in Vietnam. He was fortunate enough to escape execution and to make his way to America. Today he runs his own advertising business; but spends much of his free time traveling around the country to speak at events (at his own expense) to thank and repay American soldiers and particularly Vietnam War veterans. (I, myself, am a Vietnam Era veteran and appreciate very much what Quang does.)

Quang has a perspective on what he sees happening in our country that few of us could understand.

> *"When I was a boy of twelve in Vietnam, my father called a family meeting to tell us what was happening to our country and how we might have to run away to save ourselves. When our country fell, I was young and did as my father instructed – I ran. Many Americans died fighting for our freedom in Vietnam. Sadly, today, I must talk to my own children about possibly losing our freedom in this country; but I tell them that this time will be different. I will fight and, if I must, I will die; <u>this time I will not run</u>." – Quang Nguyen*

When I asked Quang where he stands, that is what he said. If he asked *you*, what would *you* say?

Al Lee

We the People of the United States, in Order to form a more perfect Union, establish Justice, insure domestic Tranquility, provide for the common defence, promote the general Welfare, and secure the Blessings of Liberty to ourselves and our Posterity, do ordain and establish this Constitution for the United States of America.

—Preamble to Constitution

NOTE:

A bill has been drafted and is supported by several of the newly-elected members of the US House and Senate. The bill embraces some of the proposals in this book. It should be brought up soon after the new Legislators are sworn in in 2013. I hope to publish an analysis of it before then. Watch for an announcement on www.ReformAdminLaw.org.

Thanks, Al

28. References

This book contains some ideas, opinions, and observations, and many references to events and facts to support or to illustrate them. Today's internet gives you the ability to do your own research. Please feel free to do so. To help you, I am providing some online references that you might look at. They are not in any particular order. I have tried to find references to support every claim I have made in the book and have tried to limit it to one reference per subject in the interest of brevity. I will also post all these references, plus more, on the "Links" page of the website.

Website for This Book
www•ReformAdminLaw•org

To Book Al Lee as a Speaker
Email: Al@ReformAdminLaw•org

American History
www•teachingamericanhistory•org/

Education Spending by State
http://febp•newamerica•net/k12/rankings/ppexpend

Per Pupil Spending by Country
www•dailyplunge•com/tag/per-pupil-spending-by-country/

Organisation for Economic Co-operation and Development
www•oecd•org

US Census Bureau
www•census•gov/

Federal Regulations website
http://www•regulations•gov/#!home;tab=search

Administrative Procedure Act
www•usgovinfo•about•com/library/bills/blapa•htm

Mint Confiscates Private Property
http://teapartyeconomist•com/2012/09/10/u-s-mint-keeps-80-million-in-coins-sent-to-it-for-evaluating/

Administrative Procedures Act - 1946
http://cwx•prenhall•com/bookbind/pubbooks/dye4/medialib/docs/apa1946•htm

About Federal Regulations
www•usgovinfo•about•com/od/uscongress/a/fedregulations•htm

FDA Delays Cause Deaths
http://www•ocregister•com/articles/fda-287655-drug-victims•html

The New Deal
www•u-s-history•com/pages/h1851•html

Administrative Law
www•hg•org/adm•html

US Constitution
www•usconstitution•net/const•html

Declaration of Independence
www•history•com/topics/read-the-declaration-of-independence

Social Security
www•ssa•gov

Truthful Politics
http://truthfulpolitics•com/

Social Security Disability
www•ssa•gov/disability/

Administration on Aging
www•aoa•gov/AoARoot/About/index•aspx

Jeffrey Immelt, GE, Jobs
http://www•huffingtonpost•com/2011/01/21/obama-picks-jeffrey-immel-
ge-jobs-overseas_n_812502•html

Federal Register
www•gpo•gov/fdsys/browse/collection•action?collectionCode=FR

The Road to Serfdom – F• A• Hayek
www•amazon•com/The-Road-Serfdom-Documents-The-
Definitive/dp/0226320553

NLRB Appoints ALJ
http://hr•cch•com/news/employment/091405a•asp

Heritage Foundation
www•askheritage•org

American Youth Entitlement
www•amazon•com/Cleaning-House-Twelve-Month-Experiment-
Entitlement/dp/0307730670/ref=la_B00774HTRO_1_1?ie=UTF8&qid=
1340731580&sr=1-1

Wealth of Nations – Adam Smith
www•amazon•com/Wealth-Nations-Great-Minds-
Series/dp/0879757051

Number of Federal Workers
www•numberof•net/number-of-federal-employees-2/

Cato Institute
www•cato•org/

Texas Public Policy Foundation Article—Cruz, Loyola
http://www•texaspolicy•com/center/tenth-amendment/reports/shield-
federalism-interstate-compacts-our-constitution/

Wickard v• Filburn
http://en•wikipedia•org/wiki/Wickard_v•_Filburn

Dodd-Frank
http://dealbook•nytimes•com/2010/06/28/the-dodd-frank-bill-up-close/

Davy Crockett - Welfare
www•lewrockwell•com/orig4/ellis1•html

Agenda 21
www•youtube•com/watch?v=9GykzQWlXJs

The Seventeenth Amendment
www•restorefederalism•org/?gclid=CKXu9-ufkLECFWVvTAodrixAdQ

Federalist Papers
www•foundingfathers•info/federalistpapers/

Anti-Federalist Papers
www•barefootsworld•net/antifederalist•html

Constitutional Convention - 1787
http://www•teachingamericanhistory•org/convention/

Democracy vs• Republic – Forms of Government
www•wimp•com/thegovernment/

Impact of Obamacare – Heritage Foundation

www•heritage•org/research/projects/impact-of-obamacare

Food Stamps for Illegals
http://www•fns•usda•gov/cga/factsheets/reaching•html

USDA Waste is Rampant
http://blog•heritage•org/2012/08/10/agriculture-department-pays-2-million-for-a-single-intern/?utm_source=Newsletter&utm_medium=Email&utm_content=MemberBriefing082112

Gibson Guitar Attacked by DOJ
www•redstate•com/aglanon/2011/08/31/doj-advises-gibson-guitar-to-export-labor/

Ludwig von Mises Institute
www•mises•org/

Office of Administrative Law Judges
www•oalj•dol•gov/

Totalitarian Bureaucracy
www•mises•org/daily/4585#ArticleTab

GSA Workers Mock Taxpayers
http://abcnews•go•com/GMA/video/gsa-worker-mocks-government-waste-song-cuaght-video-16085615

NOAA Goes Rogue
http://www•washingtonpost•com/opinions/george-will-blowing-the-whistle-on-leviathan/2012/07/27/gJQAAsRnEX_story•html

Sub-Prime Collapse Caused by Regulations
www•atechcorp•net/articles/article0002•aspx

US Dept• of Agriculture
www•usda•gov

US Dept• of Interior
www•doi•gov/index•cfm

US Supreme Court
www•supremecourt•gov/

Investors Business Daily
www•investors•com/offer/splash•aspx?id=subOffersKeywords&src=A8J2GPQ

Agencies Juggling Statistics
http://www•myheritage•org/news/how-the-governments-misleading-poverty-statistics-drive-welfare-spending/?utm_source=Newsletter&utm_medium=Email&utm_co
ntent=MemberBriefing082412

Horizontal Drilling
www•horizontalshaledrilling•com

Sunset Clauses-History
http://www•wisegeek•com/what-is-a-sunset-clause•htm

Hoarding and Terrorism
http://forum•prisonplanet•com/index•php?topic=223587•0

A Society Frozen in Time
www•cnn•com/2011/WORLD/americas/04/21/cuba•classic•cars/index•html

Countrywide Crony Capitalism
http://www•gopusa•com/news/2012/07/05/report-countrywide-won-influence-with-discounts/

Stimulus to Outsource Jobs
http://www•eagleforum•org/publications/column/2012-07-18•html

Tax Dollars Paid to Chinese Firms for US Infrastructure
http://abcnews•go•com/WNT/video/us-bridges-roads-built-chinese-firms-14594513?tab=9482930?ion=1206853&playlist=14594944

Advantages of Incumbency
www•cusdi•org/reelection•htm

Agency Bypassing Due Process to Seize Firearms
http://www•washingtontimes•com/news/2012/sep/6/atfs-latest-gun-grab/

Thomas Jefferson Quotes
www•famguardian•org/Subjects/Politics/ThomasJefferson/jeff1770•htm

Federalist #78
www•constitution•org/fed/federa78•htm

Woodrow Wilson and the Constitution
www•freerepublic•com/focus/f-news/2051567/posts

Farm Subsidies to Giant Agribusiness
www•heritage•org/research/reports/2002/02/farm-subsidies-are-
americas-largest-corporate-welfare-program

List Federal Law Enforcement Agencies
http://en•wikipedia•org/wiki/Federal_law_enforcement_in_the_United_
States#List_of_agencies_and_units_of_agencies

Federal Land Management
www•novapublishers•com/catalog/product_info•php?products_id=218

John Locke
http://www•thefreemanonline•org/features/john-locke-natural-rights-to-
life-liberty-and-property/

Kid Learns Lesson About Regulations
www•freedomoutpost•com/2012/08/city-shuts-down-boys-hot-dog-
stand-now-hes-homeless/

Restoring Love – Glenn Beck
www•youtube•com/watch?feature=player_embedded&v=QMErsWEo
Q9c

American War Deaths
http://www•militaryfactory•com/american_war_deaths•asp

Chick-fil-A Denied Licenses
http://godfatherpolitics•com/6318/liberal-mayors-deny-businesses-the-
right-to-operate-in-their-cities/comment-page-1/

Farm Bill Destroys Family Farms
http://news•minnesota•publicradio•org/features/200107/09_haega_sm
alltowns1/

Signers of Declaration of Independence
www•ushistory•org/declaration/signers/index•htm

Model State APA
http://www•uniformlaws•org/ActSummary•aspx?title=State%20Adminis
trative%20Procedure%20Act,%20Revised%20Model

George Orwell, 1984
www•shmoop•com/george-orwell/spanish-civil-war-wwii•html

James Lieto Property Seized from Innocent Bystanders
http://online•wsj•com/article/SB1000142405311190348090457651225
3265073870•html

California to Texas Migrations
http://www•bizjournals•com/dallas/news/2012/02/02/texas-seeing-migration-from•html

DOJ Corrupt Hiring Practices
http://www•darkgovernment•com/news/doj-biased-hiring-practices/

Void on its Face
http://sharonstephens•blogspot•com/2010/11/part-3-judgment-is-void-when-court•html

The Great Texas Banking Crash
www•amazon•com/The-Great-Texas-Banking-Crash/dp/0292727917

Burden of Regulations Grows
http://www•heritage•org/research/reports/2012/03/red-tape-rising-obama-era-regulation-at-the-three-year-mark?utm_source=Newsletter&utm_medium=Email&utm_content=MemberBriefing072712

Teachers Send Their Own Kids to Private Schools
http://hotair•com/archives/2012/09/15/almost-40-of-chicagos-public-school-teachers-send-their-kids-elsewhere-to-learn/

Dick Act – Gun Control
http://12160•info/profiles/blogs/dick-act-of-1902

Farm Bill – Heritage Foundation
http://www•heritage•org/research/factsheets/2012/09/farm-bill?query=Farm+Bill:+Ripe+for+Reform

High-Tax States Lose Residents
http://www•newsmax•com/Politics/New-York-High-Tax/2012/05/29/id/440517

Real Scientists Refute Global Warming Hoax
http://www•petitionproject•org/

29. Index